SpringerBriefs in Psychology

SpringerBriefs in Child Development

More information about this series at http://www.springer.com/series/10143

Gayle L. Macklem

Boredom in the Classroom

Addressing Student Motivation, Self-Regulation, and Engagement in Learning

 Springer

Gayle L. Macklem
Manchester, MA, USA

ISSN 2192-8363   ISSN 2192-8371 (electronic)
ISBN 978-3-319-13119-1   ISBN 978-3-319-13120-7 (eBook)
DOI 10.1007/978-3-319-13120-7
Springer Cham Heidelberg New York Dordrecht London

Library of Congress Control Number: 2014956110

Printed on acid-free paper

Springer is part of Springer Science+Business Media (www.springer.com)

Contents

Author Bios

Gayle L. Macklem is a Nationally Certified School Psychologist and a Massachusetts Licensed Educational Psychologist. She has served in the field of education for over 30 years, serving as a school psychologist/team chairperson and as an adjunct instructor in school psychology. She has developed a number of prevention programs including "The Structured Learning Program," "The Reading Initiative," "The Math Merits Program," "Project Link," and a multi-tiered program for social/emotional development. Gayle has worked as a curriculum developer and writer for the Open Circle Social Competency curriculum and is the author of *Bullying and teasing: Social power in children's groups* (2003), *A practitioner's guide to emotion regulation in school-aged children* (2008), *Evidence-based school mental health services: Affect education, emotion regulation training, and cognitive behavioral therapy (2011)*, and *Preventive mental health at school: Evidence-based services for students (2014)*. She is an instructor in the school psychology training program at the Massachusetts School of Professional Psychology in Newton, Massachusetts, where she specializes in preventive mental health; and ethics, law, and professional practices.

Chapter 1
The Academic Emotion of Boredom: *The Elephant in the Classroom*

The academic emotion of boredom, interestingly, is one of the most commonly experienced emotions of students in schools (Pekrun, Goetz, Daniels, Stupnisky, & Perry, 2010). It is not an emotion to which teachers have paid much attention. Certainly teachers have had students tell them that they are bored in class but teachers may attribute this emotion to laziness, student anxiety or depression, or to personality variables. School psychologists and other mental health personnel in schools do not have a history of either assessing or providing interventions for boredom in schools. Researchers, particularly in Germany and in Canada, have been interested in boredom for a number of years, but it is time for school professionals and particularly for school-based mental health professionals in the U.S. and other countries to become more interested in boredom as an important emotion experienced by students in our schools. Recent studies have provided school personnel a better understanding of boredom. The emotion of boredom is multidimensional and situation dependent (Acee et al., 2010). Researchers have differentiated between classroom emotions, and homework emotions, because data indicates that while emotions in both school and home settings are linked with achievement outcomes, they need to be assessed separately (Goetz et al., 2012).

The Experience of Boredom

No single variable describes boredom (Gordon, Wilkinson, McGown, & Jovanoska, 1997). Boredom has been variously described as a feeling, an emotion, an affect, a state, a drive, or a negative psychological experience (Fahlman, 2009). Boredom is experienced as a lack of activity or being disengaged from a satisfying activity. Boredom can occur during an activity and also when there is no activity in which to engage. Boredom is a negative experience rather than simply a relaxed experience. It can be mild, or unpleasant, to actually painful. The individual who is bored has

© Springer International Publishing Switzerland 2015
G.L. Macklem, *Boredom in the Classroom*, SpringerBriefs in Psychology 1,
DOI 10.1007/978-3-319-13120-7_1

difficulty paying attention, difficulty concentrating, and effort is required to maintain focus on (and not become distracted from) what is going on in the environment. Perception of time passing is also related to the experience of boredom. Fahlman describes the boredom experience as involving some combination of disengagement, dissatisfaction, inattention, altered time perception, and impaired vitality (p. 49).

Boredom has also been described as a 'silent' emotion as compared to anger for example (Fahlman, 2009), because it does not always disrupt the classroom. Boredom has been described as: 'neglected' (Fritea & Fritea, 2013; Pekrun, 2007; Pekrun et al., 2010); as 'inconsequential' (Bench & Lench, 2013); as 'poorly understood' (Malkovsky, Merrifield, Goldberg, & Danckert, 2012); as 'inconspicuous' (Goetz et al., 2014; Preckel, Götz, & Frenzel, 2010); as 'trivial' (Mercer-Lynn, Flora, Fahlman, & Eastwood, 2011); as a 'trivial annoyance' (Eastwood, Cavaliere, Fahlman, & Eastwood, 2007); 'underexplored' (Daschmann, Goetz, & Stupnisky, 2011); inconspicuous (Pekrun et al., 2010); and as receiving 'little empirical attention' (Goldberg, Eastwood, LaGuardia, & Danckert, 2011). Merrifield and Danckert (2014) label research associated with boredom as 'underdeveloped,' while Daschmann et al. writes that "much is unknown" about boredom (p. 422). Weir (2013) suggests that boredom is an 'underappreciated' emotion. Goetz et al. (2014) adds that boredom is not considered to be relevant to psychopathological diagnosis and it has no prototypical facial expression. This makes boredom the 'elephant in the classroom' (Suárez-Orozco, 2013). However, it is most certainly time for educators to pay attention to student boredom, its relevance is made very clear when the prevalence of boredom is considered.

The Prevalence of Boredom

When considering why a student may not be doing well in school, teachers, school psychologists, and counselors typically investigate a variety of variables, but it is not standard procedure to look closely at academic emotions other than test anxiety. Larson and Richards (1991) found that fifth and ninth grade students experienced boredom during 32 % of class time. Daschmann et al. (2011) determined that 44.3 % of students in grades 5–10 reported being frequently bored in math class. Nett, Goetz, and Hall (2011) reported that students in the 11th grade said they experienced boredom during 58 % of instruction time. Pekrun et al. (2010) found 42 % of undergraduate students reporting boredom in class. Daniels et al. (2009) found that students in their first year of college reported that they experienced boredom in 40 % of all academic situations.

Studies of high school students in the United States indicate that the experience of boredom is not at all unusual in school. Indiana University's 2010 High School Survey of Student Engagement (HSSSE), involving 81,000 high school students across 27 states in 2009, found that as many as 49 % of students are bored in school daily. Yazzie-Mintz (2010) used the High School Survey of Student Engagement (HSSSE) to examine student beliefs. This study involved 103 schools from 27 states, representing urban, suburban, and rural areas. The HSSSE measures cognitive engagement, social/behavioral engagement, and emotional engagement. Sixty-six percent of high school students reported that they were bored in class *every day*. One out of six students said they were bored in every class. Only 2 % said they were never bored. Eighty-one percent of students who reported boredom, felt that the class material wasn't interesting, 42 % reported the work wasn't relevant, 33 % felt work wasn't challenging, and 26 % found work too difficult. More than a third of students reported they were bored because they had no interaction with their teacher(s). This indicates that although boredom is a problem for students who may drop out of school, it is also a problem for students who stay in school. A few studies exploring boredom in specific content areas found similar results. Nett et al. (2011) found students experiencing boredom to some degree in 58 % of time spent in 11th grade math classes.

Boredom is certainly seen earlier than the high school level. A study of student emotions in seventh grade math, over a full years' time period, found whereas enjoyment and pride in mathematics declined, boredom increased over the study period (Ahmed, van der Werf, Kuyper, & Minnaert, 2013). When boredom was studied in eighth grade students as compared to 11th grade students, academic emotions were more domain specific among 11th grade students (Goetz, Frenzel, Pekrun, Hall, & Lüdtke, 2007). Older students are more likely to associate boredom in school with specific subject areas. As researchers work on developing measures of academic emotions, they are also looking at elementary aged students.

Academic Emotions

Emotion has been neglected to some extent in behavioral science and in other areas that are relevant to student performance (Seo, Barrett, & Bartunek, 2004). Emotions have affective, cognitive, physiological, and behavioral components (Daniels et al., 2009). The function of emotions is to provide information for the individual experiencing the emotion (Sansone & Thoman, 2005). A student experiences various emotions when learning, stimulated by what the students thinks about and how the student judges the situation, him/herself, the teacher, the subject, and other aspects of the learning situation (Efklides & Volet, 2005). Emotions are present before learning begins and emotions determine engagement with the task. Emotions are present at each stage of the learning process, and are present after the task has been completed and the outcome is evaluated. It is important to know what can be done to change negative effects of emotions as they relate to learning.

Until recently, *academic* emotions specifically have not received sufficient attention in school psychology or in education in general for that matter (Pekrun, Goetz, Titz, & Perry, 2002). In fact, academic emotions are considered relatively 'unexplored' (Goetz, Pekrun, Hall, & Haag, 2006, p. 289). In the past few years, the emotions experienced by students and teachers in their classrooms have drawn the attention of researchers (Pekrun & Stephens, 2009). Even with this increased interest, there have not been many research studies making strong connections to academic competence (Valiente, Swanson, & Eisenberg, 2012).

Academic emotions are those emotions that are associated with learning, classroom instruction and school achievement. They relate to activities or outcomes that relate to competence (Pekrun, Elliot, & Maier, 2009). Yet, because academic emotions affect students' quality and outcomes of learning, as well as achievement and social interactions in a school environment, exploration of academic emotions is extremely important. Academic emotions predict students' self-regulation and how they perform in the classroom (Ahmed et al., 2013). Researchers are interested in academic emotions today because academic emotions and the emotional experiences of students in learning situations are connected to their feelings of wellbeing and directly affect learning and achievement. The emotions of students in the classroom effect communication and this, in turn, affects student-teacher relationships and whether or not instruction is effective. Importantly, study of academic emotions may drive more effective interventions in that if educators can ascertain what fosters students' emotions, they may be able to develop appropriate and effective educational practices to influence outcomes.

Academic emotions include positive emotions such as enjoyment, hope, and pride; they also involve negative emotions including anger, anxiety, hopelessness, shame, and boredom (Pekrun et al., 2009). Educators do not pay very much attention to negative emotions, but academic emotions are actually quite important. Academic emotions are strongly related to students' motivation, learning strategies, self-regulation, and school achievement. Academic emotions are sometimes called 'achievement emotions' (Pekrun, Goetz, Frenzel, Barchfeld, & Perry, 2011). Achievement emotions range from enjoying learning to becoming angry when presented with challenging task demands, to experiencing boredom in class. Achievement emotions occur in class during instruction, when studying, when taking tests, and additionally during homework. Academic emotions have to do with students' success and failure, reactions to instruction, and also to the process of studying (Yan & Guoliang, 2007). Emotions stimulate action. They contribute to memory and learning (Valiente et al., 2012).

Positive and Negative Emotions

Emotions can be positive or negative. Positive emotions are difficult to observe and have not been studied to the same extent that negative emotions are studied. However, some researchers have explored the role of positive emotions in school. When students in grades 7–10 experience frequent positive emotions, they have been found to be more engaged and cope with stress more adaptively (Reschly, Huebner, Appleton, & Antaramian, 2008). Positive emotions such as enjoying learning, hopefulness, and pride support success and increase resiliency (Mega, Ronconi, & DeBeni, 2013; Shernoff, 2013). When students experience positive emotions they organize their study time, and they use summarizing skills when studying relating what they are working on to their own interests. They evaluate learning and achievement more positively and prepare for tests more strategically. They reflect on what they are learning and are more likely to believe that they can enhance their intelligence through effort. They have more confidence, believing that they are capable of achieving. Positive emotions influence self-regulated learning and mental effort (Um, Plass, Hayward, & Homer, 2012). Positive emotions increase satisfaction as well as motivation. They foster motivation to learn and use learning strategies and cognitive resources (Pekrun et al., 2002).

Recent research suggests even more specific connections between positive emotions and academic achievement. Behnardo (2013) found that enjoyment and pride predicted grades. Among students who reported lower levels of enjoyment, self-regulation was related negatively to course grades. Among students who reported higher levels of enjoyment and pride, self-regulation was positively associated with grades (Villavicencio & Bernardo, 2013). Academic emotions are related to school success and to motivation, which in turn fosters achievement. Positive emotions encourage positive appraisals of the value of doing well in courses. These relationships are understood early in development. A widely reported study of children showed that by 7 years of age children understood that positive feelings could affect cognitive performance in the classroom (Amsterlaw, Lagattuta, & Meltzoff, 2009). Joy, hope, and pride are related to academic interest and effort, and thereby affect achievement (Valiente et al., 2012). Pride in specific content areas predicts performance in those areas. A student's interest in specific content may help focus and maintain attention on schoolwork. However it should be noted that when positive emotions are of very high intensity, they interfere with achievement and even result in behavior problems.

Negative emotions have attracted more attention from researchers than positive academic emotions because they appear to have a greater effect on school outcomes. Early work suggested that negative emotions were 'bad' (Sansone & Thoman, 2005). Negative emotions can interfere with learning or it can assist and support learning. Negative emotions can improve attention and encoding (Forgas, 2013). Negative emotions can increase attention to detail, and can increase perseverance under certain circumstances.

Negative emotion in general interferes with students' grade point averages, and achievement scores (Gumora & Arsenio, 2002; Valiente et al., 2012). Even emotions connected to every-day tasks in the classroom can be problematic. However, if students also have high self-regulation, the effects of negative emotion on achievement can be ameliorated (Arsenio & Loria, 2014). A recent study of high school students showed that when students experienced higher levels of negative academic emotions and also did not cope well, their grade point averages were lower. High stress contributed to student negative academic feelings and also ineffective coping. For some learners, negative emotions can push them to work harder to avoid failure (Tulis & Fulmer, 2013).

A number of different negative emotions have been proposed to affect achievement but the academic emotion that has been studied most often is anxiety, and in particular, test anxiety (Pekrun et al., 2002). Recent research indicates that emotions affect academic performance *more* than ability or motivation (Pekrun et al., 2009). High anxiety can negatively affect attention to the task at hand (Tulis & Fulmer, 2013). It can also decrease engagement and performance when the learner is engaged in a different task.

Anxiety, in general, is associated with lower academic performance (Owens, Stevenson, Hadwin, & Norgate, 2012). Anxiety associated with learning in mathematics has drawn particular attention from researchers (Ashcraft, 2002; Faust, Ashcraft, & Fleck, 1996; Maloney, Risko, Ansari, & Fugelsang, 2010). Mazzone et al. (2007) found a statistically significant association between high levels of self-reported anxiety symptoms and poor academic performance among students 8–16 years of age; and, Wood (2006) found that changes in anxiety influenced academic and social functioning. High-stakes testing may contribute to school boredom. Studies of the impact of high-stakes testing indicate when schools focus on the high stakes test, the curricula narrows, teacher-centered approaches are more frequent, and learning activities are less varied (Mora, 2011). A small study of 30 urban, Latina/o, middle school students from grades 6 to 8 showed that students complained of boredom associated with test preparation for the test they were expected to pass. They complained their classes weren't interesting. They wanted interactive hands-on activities instead of lectures covering content that would be on the state exam.

More recently, students have been found to alternate between positive and negative motions and to experience both positive and negative emotions at the same time (Sansone & Thoman, 2005). Given this complex interplay of negative and positive emotions, patterns of emotional experiences as students engage in tasks can result in different learning outcomes. Students' emotions affect their thinking and behavior when they are trying to regulate their reactions to their environments. In addition, some of what students are trying to regulate in school *is* their emotions. At times, students can experience conflicts between their academic goals and their emotional goals.

The Negative Emotion of Boredom

Compared to anxiety, boredom does not initially appear to be psychologically relevant. However, boredom has been shown to interfere with school performance and achievement as much as anxiety (Daniels & Tze, 2014). Boredom has been described as a feeling that one has no purpose in life or meaning, and it has been explained as a result of a dull or impoverished environment (Goldberg et al., 2011). Boredom has been attributed to a student's inability to generate interest and this would make it a cognitive problem. Boredom has also been described as a motivational problem, an engagement problem, or an attentional problem. Boredom has been determined to be a distinct emotion, similar in some ways to apathy and anhedonia. It is highly correlated with depression. Boredom and depression are alike in that both are related to decreased arousal. A lack of life meaning is another way in which these negative emotions are alike. Attentional differences and memory differences are related to both depression and boredom and may be causal agents. Goldberg and colleagues were able to demonstrate that boredom and depression are indeed distinct.

Recent studies have gone beyond the effect of boredom on achievement. These studies indicate that boredom is related to: student stress, impulsivity, and risk taking; drug and alcohol use; nicotine use; depression and dissatisfaction with life; excessive gambling; impulsivity and increased risk taking; juvenile delinquency and deviant behaviors; depression; stress and distress; health problems; procrastination; increased aggression and/or anger; procrastination; and it has significant consequences leading to truancy and school dropout (Daschmann et al., 2011; LePera, 2011; Nett, Goetz, & Daniels, 2010; Orcutt, 1984; Pekrun et al., 2010; Preckel et al., 2010; Todman, 2003; Vodanovich et al., 2011; Watt & Vodanovich, 1992; Weir, 2013). In school, boredom is related to decreased motivation to perform, decreased likelihood of making an effort cognitively, reduced self-regulated learning, and decreased achievement (Preckel et al., 2010). Boredom is additionally a result of traumatic brain injury (Goldberg & Danckert, 2013). Those individuals with moderate to severe brain injury experience boredom and the need for external stimulation. Boredom is related to psychotic disorders (Todman, 2003). Among inpatients in a psychiatric hospital, those with depression experienced the highest incidence of boredom proneness (Newell, Harries, & Ayers, 2012). Boredom is related to attention deficit hyperactivity disorder (ADHD) (McKinney, Canu, & Schneider, 2013). Some individuals with ADHD experience low tolerance for boredom. Students with the inattentive type of ADHD in particular may be easily bored (Diamond, 2005; Torrente et al., 2011).

The Function of Boredom

Boredom appears to be a discrete emotion that serves a function. Boredom along with all emotions has functions. Emotions prioritize and organize our behavior in order to optimize how well we can fit with the demands of the environment (Keltner & Gross, 1999). Fredrickson (2001) suggested that positive emotions have the function of driving approach behavior; i.e., pushing an individual to engage with the environment. This is a motivational effect. In addition, positive emotions function as signals, which tell the individual to persist. Functions are the consequence of activity that is goal directed. Functional accounts of emotions treat them as complex systems of responses. Different emotions have different functions at different times. Pfister and Böhm (2008) suggest that emotions in general have four functions. The first function is to provide information, the second has to do with speed which helps individuals make rapid decisions, the third function is to direct attention to what is important at the moment, and the fourth function is commitment to action. Farb, Chapman, and Anderson (2013) identify three functions of emotions: sensory gating to filter out competing input, embodying affect, and integrating knowledge toward goal resolution.

Izard and Ackerman (2000) and Fredrickson (2001) describe the functions of the various negative emotions. Sadness allows us to slow down so that we can reflect on disappointment or failure. It lets us know that there is problem or trouble. Anger mobilizes us and helps up maintain a high degree of energy compelled by the urge to attack. Shame allows us to become aware of failures or weaknesses. Fear motivates us to escape or avoid a dangerous situation. Fear may strongly focus attention on a specific situation and give us a chance to protect ourselves. Dysfunctional negative emotions lead to discomfort or pain, motivate the person to do something that does not match his or her goals, and prevent the person from doing what is needed to reach goals (Opris & Macavei, 2005). Functional negative emotions help us pay attention to what may be blocking our goals while helping us maintain attention to these same goals. Functional negative emotions motivate us to act and encourage behaviors that are needed to reach our goals. Functional negative emotions are motivating.

Bench and Lench (2013) suggest that 'state' or temporary boredom has a function, and this function helps us establish new goals and spurs us on to explore alternatives. State boredom motivates us to seek a change. It increases arousal and motivates a desire for change thereby increasing opportunities for new stimulation. When the current situation is no longer energizing, the individual experiences decreasing emotional intensity, which also drives the individual to look for alternative experiences—even if those experiences might be negative, risky, or result in negative emotions. Any other goal at all would provide reward when the individual is experiencing boredom. Boredom therefore can encourage pursuit of new goals in a similar way that anger or frustration function to implement change. An angry individual continues to strive for a desired goal, but the bored individual only seeks change in general. The motivation that boredom provides is to drive an individual to look for alternatives.

Boredom also functions as a signal (Bench & Lench, 2013). As emotional intensity fades, boredom is introduced and signals that it is time to move to new activities. An individual's attention shifts as emotional intensity fades and boredom triggers the motivation to switch goals. When bored, the new goal simply has to be different. In this way, boredom functions as a motivator that encourages or signals action toward a new goal. Keep in mind that this function may be in relation to 'state' boredom, or boredom that is a result of external variables. Internally triggered boredom may serve different functions.

Boredom in Situations Other than at School

Boredom occurs in many situations and settings. It is experienced in leisure or free time (Barnett & Klitzing, 2006). Individuals, who are susceptible to experiencing boredom, may be as likely to experience boredom during leisure time as in learning environments. This group of individuals has difficulty becoming involved in activities especially when activities require effort. They tend to distrust others and may avoid social interaction. Introverted students and students with decreased sociability have been shown to be more likely to report boredom associated with their free or leisure time. Students who are more disorganized and those high in negative affect in general have difficulty during their free time and are more likely to report being bored. Boredom is connected to a pervasive negative affective style. Students who have difficulty finding interesting activities for themselves are more likely to experience boredom during free time as well. This is more the case among males than females in the United States. However, introversion, difficulty entertaining oneself, and emotional instability are connected to higher levels of boredom for both males and females, and for most racial and ethnic groups. This was found most strongly for Asian American, African American and Hispanic American students.

In a study of leisure boredom in South Africa, researchers followed eighth grade students for several years (Wegner, Flisher, Chikobvu, Lombard, & King, 2008). Leisure boredom predicted school dropout in students 14 year of age and older. This relationship was not found for students younger than 14. Leisure boredom is related to seeking friends in social media (Poon & Leung, 2011). An Australian study of adolescents 12–17 year of age identified less boredom in a group with structured leisure time (Fawcett, 2007). A survey of tenth grade Canadian students determined that many students, and girls in particular, experienced high levels of stress and boredom not only in school but also in leisure activities (Shaw, Caldwell, & Kleiber, 1996). Students associated boredom to a lack of options in leisure time and also to participation in activities that adults structured and led. Students shared that they participated in some leisure time activities because they wanted to please others, rather than because they were interested in the activities.

Boredom is also experienced in work situations (Fisherl, 1993). Boredom has been related to dissatisfaction with work, pay, promotion, one's work supervisor, and coworkers as well as increased absenteeism and lack of tenure (Kass, Wallace, & Vodanovich, 2003). Among adults, those high in several different types of boredom are absent more often, and are more dissatisfied with their work (Kass, Vodanovich, & Callender, 2001). Fisher (1998) found frequent disruptions increasing work-related boredom. Boredom can also occur during interpersonal situations (Orcutt, 1984). In fact Orcutt, using a scale measuring interpersonal boredom, found a relationship between this type of boredom and alcohol consumption.

Boredom in Three Academic Situations

Boredom is experienced in three academic settings to include class time, while studying, or when completing homework. Student's academic emotions associated with study and homework have had even less attention than boredom in the classroom (Goetz et al., 2012). Academic emotions experienced by students as they complete homework have not been compared to academic emotions experienced during classwork to any degree. Investigation of emotions during homework is important because the quality of students' homework has been shown to impact achievement (Dettmers, Trautwein, Lüdtke, Kunter, & Baumert, 2010). Students, who believe that their homework assignments are relevant, are more motivated. Their achievement is affected positively. When students are completing homework, their time is typically less structured and regulated by adults. At the same time, student performance remains influenced by the expectations of parents and teachers and there is a risk of critical feedback and/or negative consequences. A further difference between homework and classwork is that during homework there is no immediate social comparison as compared to the classroom situation where competition may influence performance and motivation. Some researchers have found that effort on homework was decreased among students in grade 9 as compared to earlier grades (Trautwein, Lüdtke, Kastens, & Köller, 2006). Students in grades 5–9 in general did not put as much effort into their homework as they did for their classwork, and they did not consider it as important as classwork. Among student in grades 9 and 10 who experienced negative emotions while completing their homework, effort and achievement in mathematics was decreased (Dettmers et al., 2011).

In a study of high achieving German high school students (Goetz et al., 2012), found that they could identify discrete academic emotions of students more clearly during homework as compared to identifying students discrete emotions in the classroom. Students' emotions associated with homework were less tied to work on specific subject areas, such as mathematics or English Language Arts. Self-concept/self efficacy appeared to be less important during homework than in the classroom. Researchers were able to identify differences between students' experiences during homework situations as compared to emotions experienced the classroom even though they were correlated. Older students who experienced boredom when completing homework are likely to associate this emotion with specific subject content.

Although the emotions that students experience while completing homework is of interest and is certainly relevant, this brief will specifically address the classroom situation as there is more currently known about the academic emotions in the classroom setting. In addition, educators have some direct control in regard to students' emotions in class and may be best able to address negative emotions in this environment. There is a good deal to explore in regard to boredom and subsequent chapters will address the many aspects of this common emotion gaining it's place in the study of emotions as well as in it's relation to learning, as boredom can interfere with school success and learning. A closer look at boredom is necessary given how common it is educational settings and the extent to which it affects motivation, regulated learning, and student engagement.

Chapter 2
Unmasking Boredom: *It's Not So Simple or Uninteresting—Boredom Is Both Interesting and Complex*

In order to better understand boredom, it may be helpful to determine which students may be experiencing boredom. It may also prove useful to determine in which subject areas; i.e., math, reading, etc., boredom is being experienced by students. Finally, if educators want to unmask and address boredom, those who evaluate students need to know how to measure boredom.

Ability Differences in Tendencies to Be Bored

In general, researchers who have extensively studied the experience of boredom claim that low ability and lack of achievement values relate to experiencing boredom in school (Pekrun et al., 2010). Some studies indicate that more often it is the low-ability students who report being bored, particularly at the middle school level. Bored students stop trying, withdraw effort, and may also experience high fear of failure. Their parents report that their children put little effort into homework completion. Students who describe being bored also report high fear of failure.

Experiencing boredom does not appear to be restricted to students with low ability. A study of German of sixth grade students determined that boredom was highest in students who fell in the intermediate abstract reasoning ability range (Goetz, Preckel, Pekrun, & Hall, 2007). High rates of reported boredom are also associated with high ability (Larson & Richards, 1991). In fact, in the past school psychologists and school educators suggested that boredom was due to lack of challenge in the classroom. Because academically gifted students are not a subgroup whose progress is measured by the No Child Left Behind's focus on proficiency, their needs may not be met when teachers teach to the test and they too may be bored in class (Siemer, 2009). The literature on gifted students often addresses boredom and associates this emotion with lack of challenge (Plucker et al., 2004). A small study of gifted middle school students indicated that those who did not feel challenged

© Springer International Publishing Switzerland 2015
G.L. Macklem, *Boredom in the Classroom*, SpringerBriefs in Psychology 1,
DOI 10.1007/978-3-319-13120-7_2

attended selectively and decreased effort. However in general, the question of whether or not gifted students experience boredom more frequently than their average performing, or poor performing, peers is not yet clear (Preckel et al., 2010).

In a study of ninth grade students in Austrian high school math classes, self-reports of gifted students were evaluated in regard to experiences of boredom on three occasions after being moved from mixed-ability to high-ability classrooms (Preckel et al., 2010). Once in the high ability classrooms, gifted students' self-concepts dropped significantly as might be expected due to increased competition and challenge. Researchers found differences in students' reasons for experiencing boredom in class. The group of gifted students reported that they experienced boredom due to being under challenged more often than others. Regular achieving students reported boredom due to being over-challenged more often. Once in the high ability classrooms gifted students reported boredom due to being over-challenged more often. Overall, the data suggests boredom can affect students at all levels of ability.

Gender Differences

Gender differences in tendencies to be bored have been investigated. Among college students, several studies report that men are more likely to experience boredom in academic situations than women although findings are generally mixed (Gibson & Morales, 1995; McIntosh, 2006; Sundberg, Latkin, Farmer, & Saoud, 1991). Vodanovich et al. (2011) found that men reported more boredom related to classroom instruction, environmental variables, or when perception of time and constraint was being measured as compared to women. Researchers hypothesized that males would report more boredom than females across cultures and found that this was the case only when external precursors of boredom were involved.

Yamac (2014) using a newly developed scale found that boys in fourth and fifth grades reported more boredom. A study by Lichtenfeld, Pekrun, Stupnisky, Reiss, and Murayama (2012) using a different scale with elementary school students, specifically in regard to emotions in mathematics, determined that boys in second grade reported less learning-related boredom as compared to girls. Again in relation to mathematics, third grade girls reported less enjoyment and more anxiety in all of the settings studied. Fifth grade students reported more boredom associated with class than fourth grade students.

Daschmann (2013) conducted a large study of German school students, at an average age of 12 years, in math classes. Girls reported that they were more likely to experience boredom when over challenged, when they felt that their experiences lacked meaning, and when they wished that they could be doing something else. Boys reported boredom when under challenged. In Germany as in the United States both girls and boys had similar levels of achievement in math classes, although there were self-concept and interest differences between the genders. Girls in this study did not appreciate the usefulness of mathematics and this may affect motivation to achieve, choosing to study math, and long term career choices.

Cultural and Racial Differences

Differences in boredom are typically measured by considering the tendency to experience boredom or boredom proneness, which can be thought of as a "propensity to be bored across time and situations" (Vodanovich, Verner, & Gilbride, 1991, p. 1139). In regard to cultural differences, again the studies have primarily been conducted among college age students. Boredom in learning situations has been demonstrated in both western and non-western classroom settings.

Barnett and Klitzing (2006) found that Hispanic American males tended to find their free time boring and experienced more negative than positive emotion in general. These authors found race and/or ethnicity playing somewhat more of a role than gender in regard to boredom during leisure time. Female Hispanic American university students did not experience as many positive emotions when they reported boredom proneness.

Asian American students can evidence lower self-efficacy beliefs with more fear of failure than peers (Zusho, Pintrich, & Cortina, 2005). However this does not seem to have the negative results in regard to motivation, or performance, that it does for mainstream students.

There has been *very little* attention given to the relationship of race and boredom. Watt and Vodanovich (1992) found that African American college students scored higher on a scale measuring boredom proneness. Gibson and Morales (1995) reported that African-American students report higher boredom proneness than other university students, with females scoring higher in likelihood to experience boredom.

African American middle school students can be more likely to devalue achievement as compared to other groups of students (Taylor & Graham, 2007). Among elementary level African American students, avoidance correlated with reading achievement (Guthrie, Coddington, & Wigfield, 2009). African American students who evidenced little avoidance, and again did not avoid reading tasks, achieved at high levels in reading. One reason for the connection between achievement and avoidance for African American elementary level students may be related to values. In some subgroups of African American and Hispanic boys, low-achieving boys who invest very little effort in school are admired. African American students who believed in their own ability, and could identify their own strengths, experienced higher achievement. Some African American students need assistance in self-direction and self-discipline in order to improve their motivation.

Boredom was studied among Native American adolescents from a reservation (Jervis, Spicer, & Manson, 2003). Adolescents in this study attributed boredom to social justice issues around a lack of employment or recreation. These young people coped with boredom by risk-taking and drug use. Willging, Quintero, and Lilliott (2014) were interested in the relationship of boredom to sensation seeking among Latino and White adolescents in southwestern New Mexico, where the economy was in trouble. Students associated troublemaking, particularly that of using drugs, as a coping strategy for boredom. Because some Latino youth were labeled as troublemakers, they felt demoralized. They shared that teachers, coaches, and parents told the other students to stay away from them. Boredom for alienated adolescents must be addressed to address troublemaking.

School Subject Area Differences in Triggering Boredom

Young children tend to have universal interests. They like every aspect of schooling. As children go though the grades, they develop more specific interests in various subjects that they study (Goetz, Frenzel, et al., 2007). In the case of boredom, Larson and Richards (1991) found that boredom was higher in social studies, science, and foreign language learning, as opposed to courses and subject areas such as shop, music, and gym.

Goetz, Frenzel, et al. (2007) looked at distinct academic emotions in four content areas. The emotions that they assessed were enjoyment, pride, anxiety, anger, and boredom. The content areas were mathematics, physics, German, and English. The study involved classroom emotions versus emotions during test taking or emotions during homework for eighth and eleventh grade students. Although there was a marked relation between emotions in mathematics and physics, and even stronger relations between pride in English and German, academic emotions were generally weekly connected between the subject areas. Researchers found that anger was more strongly connected to boredom as opposed to anxiety. It may be that teaching styles that do not fit students' abilities can generate both anger and boredom. Findings indicated that emotions were organized according to specific content areas, so it makes sense to talk about boredom in one content area rather than boredom in school in general.

The role of academic emotions in specific content areas or academic subject areas is important because of the relationship between academic emotions and self-regulated learning, motivation, students' interests, and choices students make that relate to making decisions toward careers (Goetz, Cronjaeger, Frenzel, Lüdtke, & Hall, 2010). In studies with German high school students, Goetz et al. (2010) found strong relationships between students' self-concept/self efficacy in mathematics, physics, English, and German. The relationship between self-concept/self efficacy and anxiety, anger, and boredom was negative, with the weakest relationship that of boredom and self-concept/self efficacy. Trait academic relations had stronger relations with self-concept/self efficacy in subject areas that were more consistent in topic and format, and were more narrowly defined or more homogenous as in mathematics and the sciences. Martin, Anderson, Bobis, Way, and Vellar (2012) were interested in student engagement and disengagement in mathematics classes, which they described as "switching on and off" (p. 1). They found mathematics anxiety in middle school students was one of the predictors of disengagement. Students who *cared strongly* about being successful in mathematics but who also felt that they would not be successful experienced the most anxiety.

Ahmed et al. (2013) studied changes in motivation, emotions, and self-regulated learning of seventh graders at three points of time in the school year in the Netherlands. Boredom increased over the time period of the study with individual differences in the rate of growth. Students who began the year with higher rates of boredom experienced faster growth of feelings of boredom as compared to their peers. Researchers were able to predict early achievement levels by measuring the four emotions of anxiety, pride, enjoyment, and boredom. The higher student anxiety and boredom initially, the lower the students' initial achievement. Over time, as the level of boredom and anxiety changed, there was a corresponding decreasing effect on achievement. Academic emotions influence a student's ability to sustain self-regulated learning. During early adolescence positive emotions decreased along with interest, liking school, in learning, and in self-esteem. As anxiety and boredom increased, achievement in mathematics decreased.

In general, students have the most negative feelings toward mathematics as compared to other subject areas in American schools (Tulis & Fulmer, 2013). Dislike of mathematics is associated with frustration while learning and with failure. When students believe that they aren't competent in a given subject areas, they experience and report more anxiety, anger, or boredom, when facing a challenging task in that subject. Tulis and Fulmer (2013) presented challenging tasks in both mathematics and in reading to middle school students. Students experienced boredom in both subjects when given challenging tasks. Boredom was related to lack of persistence in the math challenge. Students in the reading challenge who were not persistent also reported higher levels of boredom.

Goetz et al. (2006) chose to examine high performing seventh through tenth graders. They identified considerable differences in the intensity of emotions across six subject areas: i.e., Latin, English, German, mathematics, music, and sports. Students reported more enjoyment, less anxiety, and less boredom in music classes and sports, than in core subject areas. Anxiety was less specific to one subject area than enjoyment or boredom. Again these researchers provided more evidence that students' emotions were specific to each subject area, with anxiety less specific than enjoyment or boredom. Academic self-concept/self efficacy in regard to competencies in various subject areas in schools, is independent.

Time Perception in Students When Bored

Danckert and Allman (2005) hypothesized that an individual's perception of the passage of time may be a component of boredom. A class that is experienced as boring may feel as if it lasts longer than an interesting class. When a student exerts more effort over a longer time than he or she expected, the student is more likely to determine that the task is boring. The perception of time can serve as a "sensitive index of the basic function of emotion" (Droit-Volet & Meck, 2007, p. 507). When an individual's level of arousal is low, emotions push processing resources away from the student's concentration on time. The perception of time could also play a role in whether or not a student can maintain motivation when working on school tasks. If the student feels that the task has taken less time than was estimated, the student may be more motivated to continue working, and may even experience the task as enjoyable. Individuals who are high in boredom proneness make more errors when estimating time.

The perception of the passage of time was considered to be key to the experience of boredom by writers in the 1970s and students who had difficulty organizing their time were more likely to be bored (Vodanovoch et al., 2011). An earlier study of graduate students by Watt (1991) determined when presented with a boring task, students who were highly prone to boredom, experienced time passing more slowly than their peers. Wittmann and Paulis (2008) found that impulsive individuals over-estimate time duration. Children with attention deficit hyperactivity disorder may have particular difficulty processing time, tied to executive deficits (Smith, Taylor, Rogers, Newman, & Rubia, 2002). When hyperactive children were asked to deal with time reproduction tasks they appeared to have a deficit in time discrimination. The perceived slow passage of time when students are bored appears to come from the difficulty that the student has to engage in the activity at hand with full attention (Eastwood et al., 2007). Instead the student uses his attentional capacity to pay attention to *time passing* rather than the task. The passage of time becomes salient and the student feels as if time passes very slowly.

Time perception involves both duration and speed of passage (Sucala, Scheckner, & David, 2010). The difficulty of the task is also related to a student's perception of time. When students pay attention to the time passing, they perceive the time elongated, and passing slowly, when watching the clock while taking a test. Simpler tasks are perceived to take longer than more difficult tasks that require more attention. The more attentional resources that a given task demands, the greater the likelihood the student will estimate the time to pass more quickly. Having a deadline to finish a test makes the student pay attention to time. If the task is easy and there is a deadline, time passing will be overestimated. The slowest passage of time occurs when the student is aware of a time limit, and the task is easy.

Measuring Boredom

Pekrun et al. (2010) reported that as of 2010 there had been more than 1,000 studies of test anxiety in learning environments as compared to only a few studies of boredom. A serious issue for educators at the K-12 level is that the majority of research to date on boredom involves college and university-aged students. In addition, there have been concerns in the literature around the use of self-reports in studies in boredom (Bieg, Goetz, & Lipnevich, 2014; Kunter & Baumert, 2006). Some of the individuals, who report boredom using self-report measures, are the same people who have difficulty identifying their own feelings (Vogel-Walcutt, Fiorella, Carper, & Schatz, 2012). Individuals may reports boredom when they are experiencing other negative emotions. Boredom can be confused with feelings of tiredness or with inattentiveness. One way researchers try to decrease the likelihood of misattributing boredom to other emotions is to use tools with multiple questions.

In spite of their weaknesses, some researchers argue that self-reports are practical for assessing state boredom in school situations (Vogel-Walcutt et al., 2012). In fact, student self-perceptions may be valid. Pekrun et al. (2010) suggest that the self-report "seems to be the best method available for assessing achievement emotion" (p. 546). Daschmann (2013) argues that student perceptions of feelings (emotions perceived subjectively) can be assumed to have high validity when they are compared to parents', teachers', or others' observations. Kunter and Baumert (2006) used questionnaires to examine aspects of instruction in German classrooms and determined that student ratings could indeed tap different aspects of the learning environment. Subjective measures of boredom may actually help teachers identify learning material and instruction strategies that contribute to boredom in the classroom (Vogel-Walcutt et al., 2012).

Academic Emotions Questionnaires

A relatively new scale to measure academic emotions has been developed by Pekrun et al. (2011). This scale has been described as the first scale to measure academic or achievement emotions. The Achievement Emotions Questionnaire (AEQ) is based on a more complex definition of achievement emotions than previous measurement attempts. This scale includes 24 scales measuring nine different emotions in three academic settings. The nine different emotions include: Enjoyment, hope, pride, relief, anger, anxiety, hopelessness, shame, and boredom (p. 38). The emotions chosen for this scale are common and are frequently reported by students. The situations included are class-related, learning-related, and test-related. The scale is intended to measure trait or habitual versus state emotions. The authors indicate that changing the instructions for the questionnaire would allow the scale to measure either state emotions or course-specific emotions. The tool was evaluated in a sample of university students. Item reliabilities were deemed good to excellent. Internal structural validity was determined to be adequate. The emotions measured in this very comprehensive scale were distinct individually and across the three settings. Hopelessness and boredom had negative correlations with intrinsic motivation, effort, self-regulation and academic performance (p. 45). The scale, at this point, is too long for practical application.

An important development for those working with children is the development of an elementary-school version of the Achievement Emotions Questionnaire (Lichtenfeld et al., 2012). This tool measures only three emotions and three types of academic settings. The three emotions are enjoyment, anxiety, and boredom, all very important at the elementary-school level. The three settings include attending class, completing homework, and test taking. The tool has been tested on both American and German school students. A study involving German students demonstrated the reliability and structural validity of the tool. A second study involving

American students was able to demonstrate cross-cultural validity. This tool may be very useful for school psychologists and others working in public schools in at least the two countries already involved in research studies. Yamac (2014) reported information about a different tool designed to measure enjoyment, anxiety, and boredom in students in the classroom at the elementary level. This 34-item tool was studied in a Turkish elementary school in the fourth and fifth grades. The current version of the tool was demonstrated to be composed of three factors with satisfactory reliability and high internal consistency. Boredom using this scale correlated positively with anxiety.

More Specific Measures of Boredom

The first measure of 'state' boredom was developed by Fahlman, Mercer-Lynn, Flora, and Eastwood (2013). The Multidimensional State Boredom Scale (MSBS) has five factors to include disengagement, high arousal, low arousal, inattention, and time perception. Scores on this scale were correlated with trait boredom. Scores were also correlated with depression, anxiety, anger, inattention, impulsivity, neuroticism, life satisfaction, and purpose in life. A second-order factor was identified as 'general boredom' (Fahlman, 2009). The 29-item MSBS was found to significantly correlate with the Boredom Proneness Scale.

Acee et al. (2010) administered the Academic Emotions Questionnaire and an Academic Boredom Scale consisting of 36 items. From these, they derived a 10-item Academic Boredom Scale with strong reliability and validity coefficients. They also found a single general boredom factor in situations in which students reported being under-challenged; but for students who said they were over-challenged, a two boredom factor model fit better. Task-related boredom was perceived as tedious and meaningless. Self-focused boredom was described as baffling, frustrating, and dissatisfying.

There have been a number of attempts to measure boredom as it relates to learning situations. Of these, there are two popular measures (Goldberg et al., 2011; Mercer-Lynn et al., 2011). One is the Boredom Proneness Scale (BPS) by Farmer and Sundberg (1986), and the other is the Boredom Susceptibility Scale (ZBS) by Zuckerman (1979). These two scales have received considerable attention in the literature.

The Boredom Susceptibility Scale (ZBS) was first published as a subscale of Zuckerman's Sensation Seeking Scale (Zuckerman, 1979, 2007; Zuckerman, Eysenck, & Eysenck, 1978; Zuckerman, Kolin, Price, & Zoob, 1964). The ZBS measures "the inability to tolerate monotonous environmental stimulation…an aversion to repetition, routine…." (Zuckerman et al., 1978, p. 140). This 18-item scale considers boredom a trait, in spite of criticism that the majority of items reflect boredom related to the environment. The subscale has ten pairs of forced-choice items and correlates with extraversion, risky behaviors, drug use, and risky driving. A recent study of the Sensation-Seeking Scale in Italian high school and college age students suggested some issues with the factorial structure of the scale. Of relevance here, the Boredom Susceptibility subscale had low reliability in this particular sample (Manna, Faraci, & Como, 2013). However, samples of American college students have demonstrated adequate reliability and strong validity (Vodanovich, 2003).

Goldberg et al. (2011) consider the Boredom Proneness Scale, the "only empirically validated, comprehensive tool for measuring boredom" (p. 649). The Boredom Proneness Scale consists of 28 items with responses arranged in a 7-point Likert scale ranging from '1' (highly disagree) to '7' (highly agree) (Sommers & Vodanovich, 2000). A high score is interpreted as high boredom proneness. Test-retest reliability and internal consistency along with construct validity have been determined to be adequate. The scale is a self-report questionnaire. The scale has two factors, lack of external stimulation and lack of internal stimulation (Farmer & Sundberg, 1986; Goldberg et al., 2011; Vodanovich & Kass, 1990; Vodanovich, Wallace, & Kass, 2005). The External Stimulation subscale deals with a need for variety and change. The Internal Stimulation subscale explores perceived inability to produce stimulation for one's self. Others have identified up to five factors (Vodanovich, 2003), although there is more agreement in the research for two factors. Correlates of the Boredom Proneness Scale include negative affect and differences in cognition and attention. The BPS is considered useful in separating boredom from other negative feelings. The wide-ranging research on boredom proneness shows a relationship with a variety of behaviors, dispositions, and personality variables.

The Same or Different Constructs?

Apparently both the Boredom Proneness Scale and the Boredom Susceptibility Scale were thought to measure trait boredom originally, but they do not seem to measure the same construct (Mercer-Lynn et al., 2011). The two scales have been found to be associated with different outcomes. The Boredom Proneness Scale appears to measure more internalizing issues. The Boredom Susceptibility Scale measures externalizing problems for the most part. The scales may both be measuring difference types or aspects of trait boredom. Mercer (2008) pointed out that although there is some overlap between the scales, there are significant differences between the scales. The Boredom Proneness Scale appears to address negative affect, attentional difficulties, and lack of connection with the environment or others. The Boredom Susceptibility Scale appears to measure a need for excitement, motor or behavioral impulsivity, and a need for stimulation. The Boredom Proneness Scale predicts sensitivity to punishment and lowered sensation seeking. The Boredom Susceptibility Scale predicts increased reward sensitivity and sensation seeking.

Research has identified a difference between the scales in regard to behavioral activation and behavioral inhibition (Mercer-Lynn, Bar, & Eastwood, 2014; Mercer-Lynn et al., 2011; Mercer-Lynn, Hunter, & Eastwood, 2013). The behavioral *inhibition* system correlates with Boredom Proneness Scale. This system regulates avoidance behavior in the individual. Behaviorally inhibited students are more likely to experience boredom when the situation is in fact boring. This suggests that the setting and the person *interact* to cause the experience of boredom. The behavioral inhibition system predicts 'state' boredom in boring situations. Students more, sensitive to punishment are more likely to experience boredom in monotonous or low stimulation settings. The behavioral *activation* system is correlated with the Boredom Susceptibility Scale. The behavioral activation system regulates approach behaviors. Given these differences, the two scales may interact with settings inducing boredom differently. Boredom may involve a conflict between "an aversive state of being unable to attentionally engage and an approach motivation of wanting/needing to engage" (Mercer-Lynn et al., 2014, p. 125).

It also appears that the Boredom Proneness Scale measures two distinct forms of boredom tendencies (Dahlen, Martin, Ragan, & Kuhlman, 2005). One form is related to lack of internal stimulation and the other lack of external stimulation (Vodanovich et al., 2005). The items on the External Stimulation subscale have to do with a need for variety and change. The items on the Internal Stimulation subscale measures perceived inability to internally create sufficient stimulation. Vodanovich et al. attempted to revise the Boredom Proneness Scale by performing a confirmatory factor analysis. This resulted in a short-form, 12-item version, of the Boredom Proneness Scale with increased reliability. The authors expect that if educators can identify more distinct reasons for student boredom, they can design more appropriate interventions. Given no gender differences were identified, the scale (BPS-SF; i.e. short form) may be quite useful. Boredom proneness is related more closely to attentional impulsivity, avoidance, and other negative emotions (Mercer-Lynn et al., 2013). Boredom susceptibility appears to be related to motor impulsivity.

Chapter 3
The Many Faces of Boredom: *A Negative Emotion That Is So Common, It Is Simply Accepted, or Brushed Off*

Researchers have attempted to dissect the complex concept of boredom in a number of different ways. One way to understand the complexity of the emotion of boredom is to look at *task-focused* boredom as compared to *self-focused* boredom (Acee et al., 2010). Task-focused boredom occurs when students are faced with a meaningless task. Self-focused boredom occurs when the student feels frustrated. Neu (1998) described *endogenous* versus *reactive* boredom. Endogenous boredom would be boredom generated from within the individual. Reactive boredom would be boredom in reaction to what was going on in the environment. Weir (2013) wrote that boredom can generate lethargy or it can generate agitation. In a classroom some students may look as if they are dozing while others maybe wiggling in their seats. Researchers have described these manifestations of boredom as 'apathetic' and 'agitated' (Malkovsky et al., 2012). Clearly boredom has different faces and these had been addressed in the literature on boredom.

State Boredom

Researchers propose that boredom can be considered a 'trait,' or boredom can be experienced as a 'state' (Vogel-Walcutt et al., 2012). It is common to find the terms boredom proneness and boredom when a writer refers to two different types of boredom in the same article (Todman, 2013).

There has been quite a bit of study considering boredom a 'state.' This may be the most studied way in which researchers have addressed the many faces of boredom. When considering boredom as a state, the student's perception of the immediate environment is key (Bench & Lench, 2013). State boredom occurs when the student perceives that the classroom, homework, or free-time activity, is not sufficiently stimulating. Experiencing boredom signals the student that he or she should look for a different goal or experience. This could have negative results in a

© Springer International Publishing Switzerland 2015
G.L. Macklem, *Boredom in the Classroom*, SpringerBriefs in Psychology 1,
DOI 10.1007/978-3-319-13120-7_3

Table 3.1 Antecedents of state boredom

• Students' perceptions that a given task or piece of work is meaningless
• Students' reacting to tasks in which there is insufficient direction
• Tasks for which resources are inadequate
• Restrictive situations (students cannot leave class)
• Learning situations during which students have very little control
• Tasks that are disliked and students would rather be doing something else
• Teaching approaches that are not exciting or stimulating
• Teaching that does not match students' skill or ability levels
• When goals are not clear or focused

Source: Vogel-Walcutt et al. (2012, p. 103)

classroom should a student decide to become disruptive to increase stimulation. However, the fact that boredom can signal behavior suggests that boredom may have a function. State boredom may be a temporary experience that occurs in reaction to what is, or is not, going on around the individual (Fahlman, 2009). This implies that boredom could be experienced by anyone as a reaction to a setting that is not stimulating. State boredom fluctuates over time, or over a school day. State boredom is a result of the neurological state of low arousal. It is a negative psychological state in reaction to low arousal such as dissatisfaction, frustration, or disinterest (Vogel-Walcutt et al., 2012). In this sense, boredom consists of both arousal and disinterest.

Blunt and Pychyl (1998) examined the relationship between state boredom and procrastination in an undergraduate population. They found that avoidance and procrastination in making decisions related to both state orientation and proneness to boredom. Vogel-Walcutt et al. (2012, p. 103) have identified a variety of antecedents of state boredom (Table 3.1).

Vogel-Walcutt et al. (2012) reviewed the extant literature on 'state' boredom in order to derive a definition that would move the research forward. They examined the literature that considered boredom an unpleasant feeling stimulated by the environment, and also the works that described boredom as temporary feelings of low energy and disinterest. They also examined the literature that addressed both aspects. It seems that feelings of boredom are triggered when a learner believes that the task at hand has no meaning for him or her. Feelings of boredom many be generated when a task is monotonous, repetitive, and/or unexciting. These feelings may arise when the learner is faced with work that is too easy, or too difficult, and when the learner has no control of over the process of learning. The learner may feel uninterested and tired. This feeling is best described as 'low arousal.' Vogel-Walcutt and colleagues determined that boredom is the interaction of low levels of arousal along with emotions that are experienced as unpleasant. State boredom strongly impacts learning in a negative manner as might be expected.

Recently, Fahlman et al. (2013) published the first measure of 'state' boredom. This scale measures five factors: i.e., disengagement, high arousal, low arousal, inattention, and time perception. No differences between males and females have been found using this scale, and scores correlated with a variety of variables to include: trait boredom, other negative emotions, inattention, impulsivity, neuroticism, life satisfaction, and purpose in life.

Trait Boredom

Trait boredom is typically described as *boredom proneness* or increased susceptibility to boredom. This is a characteristic of some individuals. An individual, who is prone to boredom, is more likely to experience negative affect than positive affect (Barnett & Klitzing, 2006). Boredom proneness has additionally been associated with a wide range of problems. Individuals high in boredom proneness also experience more anger and aggression, along with difficulty controlling their anger (Dahlen, Martin, Ragan, & Kuhlman, 2004; Rupp & Vodanovich, 1997). High boredom proneness is closely tied to difficulty holding anger in when it has been triggered. When boredom prone individuals were exposed to an environment with low stimulation, anger was a likely outcome. External boredom proneness, but not internal boredom proneness, triggers anger when an individual is bored. Those individuals, who experienced boredom as a result of an environment with little stimulation, were more impulsive than their peers. They sought more novelty and excitement. Researchers suggested that internal boredom proneness appears to be a different construct than external boredom proneness.

Boredom proneness is associated with extraversion (Gordon et al., 1997). It has been shown to be associated with decreased achievement, truancy, abuse of drugs and alcohol, and eating disorders (Sommers & Vodanovich, 2000). Individuals who are particularly susceptible to boredom tend to report more health symptoms and somatization. Their feelings are more easily hurt, they tend to be shy, and feel that others don't like them. Boredom proneness is associated with impulsiveness (Watt & Vodanovich, 1992); with mood monitoring (Harris, 2000); with introspectiveness (Gana, Deletang, & Metais, 2000); with several subtypes of pathological gambling (Blaszczynski, McConaghy, & Frankova, 1990); and with anxiety, hopelessness, loneliness, and depression (LePera, 2011; Sommers & Vodanovich, 2000). Those individuals high in boredom proneness tend to report greater frequency of psychological symptoms. Trait boredom uniquely predicts depression (Carriere, Cheyne, & Smilek, 2008; Mercer-Lynn et al., 2014). Clinicians believe that attentional problems are a result of depression and have developed coping treatments for depression that address attention training (Abramson, Metalsky, & Alloy, 1989; Hollon, Haman, & Brown, 2002; Papageorgiou & Wells, 2000).

In adults, boredom proneness is related to perceptions of being underemployed (Watt & Hargis, 2010). These adults did not feel that they were supported by their organizations. They felt that their supervisors evaluated them less positively than others. Individuals high in boredom proneness tend to hold external work values, which relate to careers (Vodanovich, Weddle, & Piotrowski, 1997). This is important information for those involved in adolescent guidance. Boredom is clearly a problem in the workplace as well as in the schools. Also among adults, boredom proneness predicted hyperactivity, feelings that time passes slowly, and sleep problems (Kass, Wallace, & Vodanovich, 2003). Wallace, Vodanovich, and Restino (2003) identified a connection between sleepiness during the day and boredom proneness in undergraduate and military groups. Together, these behaviors in turn predicted cognitive failure and attention deficit disorder.

An earlier study by Leong and Schneller (1993) investigated risks related to boredom proneness. Highly dogmatic individuals with low persistence were more susceptible to boredom. These individuals were also less social and had difficulty inhibiting impulsivity. Although the study involved college-aged students, a tendency toward boredom (boredom proneness), was related to risky and aggressive driving, expressing anger while driving, and taking risks while driving, along with impulsiveness and sensation seeking (Dahlen et al., 2005).

Combined State and Trait Boredom

Although some researchers consider trait and state boredom as different (Bench & Lench, 2013), state and trait differences appear to be confounded. Fahlman (2009) argues that every experience of boredom is always a combination of internal and external variables. Boredom occurs in the relationship between the person and their interpretation of their experience. Both the internal experience and the external environment is important. Both contribute to both state and trait boredom.

State and trait boredom have not been assessed in the same study very often. Todman (2013) designed a self-report measure designed to inventory feelings and thoughts about boredom experiences during the past 14 days. The tool assessed boredom experiences using eight questions about different aspects of the experience. Students responded using a 7-point Likert scale. A summary score was out of the question in that questions involved different judgments. All items had significant positive correlations with the Boredom Proneness Scale (BPS; Farmer & Sundberg, 1986) and a less strong association with the Boredom Susceptibility Scale. The student's relationship with the learning environment that generates feelings of boredom can be externally or internally triggered. The degree of mismatch varies greatly among individual students. Because tolerance for boredom in an unrewarding environment differs among students, and because there are differences in students' perceptions of whether or not the environment is in fact unrewarding, trait boredom measures alone cannot predict boredom.

Subtypes of Boredom

Goetz et al. (2014) consider boredom the most intense and most often perceived academic emotion. In a seminal study of 11th grade high school students and college students, researchers identified five types of boredom described below.

- *Indifferent boredom* (possibly pleasant feeling).
  Students experiencing *indifferent boredom* have been described as cheerfully fatigued, relaxed, or even withdrawn. In the high school sample, only 11 % of students indicated that they experienced this type of boredom and it was the least commonly experienced subtype overall.
- *Calibrating boredom* (daydreaming without any motivation to change).
  Students experiencing the *calibrating* type of boredom report wandering thoughts. They do not appear to know what to do, are uncertain, and are eager to change the situation or setting. They are apt to begin thinking about things that are off-target, or off-topic. This subtype of boredom is somewhat unpleasant but not excessively so. A student experiencing this subtype would go along with an alternative activity although may not actively look for something different.
- *Searching boredom* (effortful to change the situation).
  Students experiencing the *searching* subtype are restless and actively look for something different. They are aware that they need activity and may begin to think about other interests. This type of boredom is unpleasant.
- *Reactant boredom* (trapped, angry feelings).
  Students experiencing the *reactant* subtype are strongly motivated to escape boredom. They are restless, may be angry or aggressive, and are very uncomfortable. This type is particularly unpleasant and aversive. Clearly arousal for this subtype is high. These students may blame the setting, the teacher, the subject, or the materials, all of which are perceived to be inducing the feelings of boredom.
- *Apathetic boredom* (unmotivated).
  Students experiencing *apathetic* boredom had low levels of both positive and negative emotions. They were dissatisfied and helpless. The feelings associated with *apathetic* boredom were extremely unpleasant. In this study, high school students reported more boredom than the college students. In fact *apathetic* boredom was especially high in the high school sample where it encompassed 36 % of reported boredom experiences.

The different subtypes are characterized by different intensities of boredom, with *indifferent* boredom milder, and less intense, as compared to the others. Goetz et al. (2014) argue that *reactant* boredom is most associated with schooling; whereas, *indifferent* boredom may be more closely related to leisure or free time. Researchers have been able to provide some support for the external validity of the several subtypes. In a study with both high school and university students in Germany, Goetz and colleagues determined that students experiencing *indifferent* boredom were the least impacted; whereas, those experiencing *reactive* boredom had the most negative profiles. The latter experienced high negative emotions with elevated anger. An unexpected finding was the latest subtype, which researchers labeled *apathetic*. Goetz and Frenzel (2006), who first proposed different subtypes, had not identified this subtype. *Reactant* and *apathetic* boredom subtypes were reported most often in school environments. *Apathetic* boredom was similar to learned helplessness and/or depression.

Goetz et al. (2014) concluded that students experience specific types of boredom and therefore boredom could be best described as 'multiple boredoms.' However, whether the different subtypes are related to dispositions or the environment had not been determined as of 2013–2014, although researchers suggest that extroverts may be more likely to fit in the *reactant* boredom subtype when they find themselves in situations from which they cannot escape or change.

Several researchers have examined several of these different types of boredom further. *Searching* boredom seems to be related to creativity although this is not likely to be observed in the school context (Nett et al., 2011). A student experiencing *apathetic* boredom may gives the impression that he or she simply doesn't care about the content being presented (Malkovsky et al., 2012). *Apathetic* boredom is connected to lapses in attention in class, even to difficulty keeping one's eyes open (Weir, 2013). Bored students have difficulty mustering up the effort needed to concentrate. Boredom can also cause restlessness as a result of efforts to sustain attention. '*Agitated boredom*' (Goetz et al.'s (2014) *reactant boredom*) is associated with symptoms of attention deficit disorder (tapping one's feet) and is related to difficulties with sustained attention. Boredom can undoubtedly lead to agitation and anger if a student cannot escape a situation he/she considers boring.

An interesting study conducted by Baker, D'Mello, Rodrigo, and Graesser (2010) involving three different computer-based learning situations with high school and college students may contribute to the understanding of how agitated boredom might affect learning. These researchers found that in three different learning situations, with different populations of students, and using different methods, the most persistent emotion was boredom. Bored students tended to 'game the system,' which involved 'guessing' in order to perform well without learning the material. This study, using situations which might be expected to hold students interest, found that once a student felt bored, this emotional state was very difficult to change and resulted in significantly less learning and mastery. The researchers recommend that boredom be detected early in learning situations and that adults respond quickly to change students' emotions. They strongly argue that educators try to *prevent* boredom before it occurs.

Chapter 4
Theory: *What Is Causing Our Students to Tune Out and Turn Off?*

Boredom is quickly becoming, or more likely has already become, a serious subject of study. All serious subjects of study need to rely on theories. Theory explains why students act. Theory provides a way to think about the topic of interest (Macklem, 2014). Theory helps us understand what should be researched and helps us design and interpret research studies (Kelly, 2010). Theory contributes to what is already known about a topic. Theory helps us ask important questions.

Earlier Theories

Larson and Richards (1991) provided several interesting models of boredom. Research on boredom has attributed the feeling of boredom to under-stimulation. It could occur in any situation characterized by repetition and lack of challenge, in which case the student or worker would experience under-arousal. Subsequent studies showed individuals also become bored when engaged in complex tasks or when students were anxious. This led to a model of boredom which was designated the forced-effort model (Hill & Perkins, 1985).

The forced-effort model conceptualized boredom as a result of being forced to invest mental effort on a task that the person felt was monotonous and became frustrated (Hill & Perkins, 1985). The idea here was that boredom would be experienced in teacher-directed activities where students have little control of their own learning. Students prone to boredom would need to work harder than their classmates on everyday schoolwork. This group of students would be more likely experience depression, and would be less well adjusted than their peers.

A second model conceived of boredom as a social construction (Larson & Richards, 1991). Frequent boredom in high school was hypothesized to be associated with resistance to school authority. If a student claimed that he or she were bored the situation could be blamed on the teacher, in that the teacher had not

© Springer International Publishing Switzerland 2015
G.L. Macklem, *Boredom in the Classroom*, SpringerBriefs in Psychology 1,
DOI 10.1007/978-3-319-13120-7_4

provided work that had a purpose or meaning. A third model, the resistance model, suggested that boredom was related to the presence of adult control.

The three models described by Larson and Richards (1991); i.e., under-stimulation, forced effort, and resistance, were studied in a sample of fifth to ninth grade students. Researchers found that boredom occurred frequently in all activities for this age group, although boredom was at its highest during schoolwork—and particularly during those situations in which teachers directed the activities. During classwork, students reported that their boredom was related to the fact that they didn't like their classes. Both the forced-effort and resistance models would account for this situation. Outside of school, during leisure, students explained boredom as a result of having nothing to do. The under-stimulation model would account for this experience. In the Larson and Richards study, boredom did not increase in the junior high years and was not characterized by any one group of students, such as those who were underachieving or highly competent students. Both high ability students and oppositional students reported boredom as they completed their schoolwork.

Dimensional Models

More recently, researchers have differentiated and categorized emotions according to two or three dimensions. One model differentiates academic emotions along two dimensions (Tulis & Fulmer, 2013). One dimension is that of *valence*; i.e., positive emotions versus negative emotions. The other is *activation*, i.e., activating as compared to deactivating. Boredom is a deactivating emotion (Pekrun et al., 2010). It is also negative. Boredom is associated with disengagement and lower performance in a school situation.

However if a student is bored long enough, the student's activity level may increase as a result of trying to sustain attention or dealing with anger generated when a situation cannot be changed (Pekrun et al., 2010). In this case, boredom can activate arousal and behavior.

Activating emotions, whether they are positive or negative, have been demonstrated to help students persist on tasks under certain circumstances (Tulis & Fulmer, 2013). Negative emotions tend to effect students by signaling that the task at hand is a problem and action is necessary. This suggests that both positive and negative emotions serve motivating functions, anxiety in particular. Boredom may not have the same effect, which suggests that teachers need to distinguish between boredom and anxiety in their students.

The Control-Value Theory of Achievement Emotions

Pekrun (2006) developed a *control-value theory of achievement emotions* to explain the effects of boredom on academics. Pekrun et al. (2010) describe boredom in the same manner as other achievement emotions, according to valence and activation.

Valence refers to whether or not the emotion is positive and pleasant or negative and unpleasant to painful. In addition, they describe emotions as activating and driving action or deactivating, which might result in emotional withdrawal. Studies indicate that fifth and sixth graders do withdraw effort when they experience boredom, feel helpless, or are angry with the teacher (Jarvis & Seifert, 2002).

According to the control-value theory, students' appraisals of both control and value predict their emotional experiences (Pekrun, 2006; Tulis & Fulmer, 2013). Students experience academic emotions when they feel that they are in control, or are out of control, of their schoolwork and when *they care* about doing well. Caring about the work is also important. If students don't find the work interesting, and also feel that the work is of little value to them, they experience boredom. Because boredom causes a student to reduce attention to the work that the student feels is of little value, the student will become distracted and will think of something other than the task at hand. The academic task is experienced as aversive and the goal of the student becomes avoidance. Boredom instigates a desire to escape from the situation (Pekrun et al., 2010). In school settings this could be manifested as daydreaming or disruption. The function of boredom then is to pull one's attention from the activity that is perceived as unrewarding, and lacks value. This reduces cognitive focus by directing attention to something more rewarding through distraction, or daydreaming, or misbehavior. The students' motivation is avoidance or passivity. Effort is reduced, and investment in more complex thinking is negatively affected.

In a series of studies, Pekrun et al. (2010) demonstrated that boredom had a significant negative effect on performance and grades, even when controlling for prior achievement. Students experience distinct emotions when they subjectively feel that they are in control or when they feel out of control of the activity, task, or setting. Pekrun et al. (2010) described subjective control as "the perceived causal influence on an agent over actions and outcomes" (p. 534). A student may also feel the course material isn't stimulating and therefore won't care very much about whether he/she will master the content; i.e. the student may not subjectively value the course content. Pekrun et al. describe subjective value as "the perceived valences of actions and outcomes" (p. 534). A student experiences negative emotions when he/she believes that an examination is very important, and in addition, the student does not feel that he or she can control the outcome of the exam. Both subjective feels are involved. This student will experience boredom.

Boredom acts to withdraw attention from the task at hand (Pekrun et al., 2010). It causes a student to work to distract herself and the result is paying attention to something other than what is going on in the classroom, or other than what the teacher may be presenting. Talking with a classmate may be more stimulating and carry a higher value. Boredom reduces academic motivation. It affects achievement by causing a student to process information in a cursory manner (shallow). It diminishes the chance that the student will use flexible problem-solving strategies and fosters a passive approach to studying or classroom learning. Boredom is therefore deactivating in that it decreases concentration and decreases effort. It additionally increases distractibility and causes attention problems.

The control-value theory suggests that students' emotions can be effected by whether or not the student feels competent and in control over his or her achievement

(Pekrun et al., 2009). This theory also suggests that students' emotions can be effected by whether or not the student feels that he or she can control the outcome of efforts in the classroom. Emotions can also be influenced, by changing whether or not the student values activities of the classroom. The control-value theory therefore suggests a number of ways that educators may influence whether or not the students perceive classes as interesting or boring.

The Attentional Theory of Boredom Proneness

The *attentional theory of boredom proneness* proposes that boredom results from a deficit in attention (Harris, 2000; LePera, 2011). Cognitive theorists have suggested for some time that individuals who are prone to be bored have an individual difference in their ability to self-regulate attention. According to this theory boredom is caused by a failure of attentional processes (Eastwood et al., 2007). Attention can be part of the definition of boredom and also be a cause of boredom. Fisher (1993) argues that the amount of stimulation, that various individuals feel they need, varies considerably. It varies between various individuals, it varies over time, it varies according to the person's age, and it varies according to a person's personality. Stimulation depends on a person's perception rather than on the situation at hand. What may be considered boring by the individual depends on that person's interests, concerns, and values. Individual differences in ability to attend interacts with cognitive demands of the task at hand resulting in boredom. The individual, who is not able to self-regulate attention, will experience boredom (Mercer-Lynn et al., 2014).

Inattention is thought to be one of a number of components of boredom. Self-awareness of attention may be particularly important (Damrad-Frye & Laird, 1989). Students who attend less well as compared to peers, and who have poor attentional control, tend to be the students who report boredom in the classroom (Barnett & Klitzing, 2006). Studies show that boredom decreases attention to schoolwork (Larson & Richards, 1991). A study of German college-aged students demonstrated that boredom actually *causes* attention problems (Pekrun et al., 2010).

Tasks that a student could finish without focused attention can be easily affected by distraction (Eastwood et al., 2007). If the task itself doesn't encourage sustained attention, the student must generate self-sustained attention and this could be experienced as boring. Boredom, according to attention theories, considered an inability to engage and sustain attention (Carriere et al., 2008). People who are highly prone to experiencing boredom perform poorly on measures of sustained attention (Malkovsky et al., 2012). There are wide differences in individuals' boredom proneness as a consequence of their ability to be attentive when working on tasks in school or at work. When an individual experiences a chronic inability to engage and sustain attention; interest decreases, there is loss of meaning in the tasks, motivation decreases, and negative emotions become persistent (Cheyne, Carriere, & Smilek, 2006). This is experienced as boredom.

Eastwood, Frischen, Fenske, and Smilek (2012) have defined boredom in terms of attention in that it is experienced when a person is unable, yet aware, of his or her inability to activate the degree of attention needed to successfully engage in an activity that has the potential to be rewarding. The individual blames the perceived cause of boredom rather than any internal disability. This theory suggests that students experience boredom: when they have difficulty paying attention to their own thoughts or feelings; when they have difficulty attending to the environments; when they are aware that they are having difficulty paying attention; and when they believe that the environment is causing them to feel bad or dissatisfied.

Most studies that examine the connection between boredom and attention are correlational studies (Eastwood et al., 2007). In a study of boredom and sustained attention, researchers described two of the ways that boredom can be experienced (Malkovsky et al., 2012): *agitated* and *apathetic*. Individuals who experience *apathetic* boredom, are not interested in activities but at the same time are not motivated to do anything about this, such as trying to change either their feelings or the situation. Individuals who experience agitated boredom try to find an activity that is more interesting, although they are not likely to find something that is satisfying. These two groups of individuals appear to be distinctly different in regard to personality, novelty or sensation seeking, and sustained attention. This suggests that there may be two types of boredom proneness. The apathetic boredom-prone individual is not motivated to engage in what maybe going on; and the agitated boredom-prone individual, who is motivated albeit unsuccessfully. The apathetic boredom-prone individual experiences lapses in attention whereas the agitated boredom-prone individual does not. The attentional characteristics of the agitated boredom-prone individual are similar to individuals with ADHD. They are more attentive than those with apathetic boredom-proneness, but their attentional difficulties include: errors of sustained attention, increased activity levels, impulsivity, and negative affect. This research further delineates subtypes of boredom described in the previous chapter.

Researchers interested in attention have further explored attention lapses and mind wandering. Using a brief self-report scale to assess classroom performance difficulties connected with problems sustaining attention, these researchers found that boredom proneness was a consequence of attention lapses (Cheyne et al., 2006). Attention lapses cause errors as a separate consequence. Researchers felt that even brief lapses in attention could have consequences involving a student's ability to remain motivated and persist in completing school tasks. And, a student's ability to enjoy tasks would be affected as well. Mind-wandering thoughts may be triggered by boredom (Kane & McVay, 2012). In a study of college students, Carriere et al. (2008) found that memory deficits along with attentional deficits contribute to feelings of boredom. When tasks are undemanding, students with stronger working memory abilities actually experience more mind wandering than students with less working memory capacity. Working memory acts to suppress unrelated mind wandering thoughts when tasks demand attention. When tasks do not demand attention, students may be more susceptible to mind wandering. An individual's attention-control capability accounts for mind-wandering and working memory. Interestingly, when the student in a classroom is engaged in satisfying mind-wandering, the student may not feel bored, although he is likely to say later that the task was boring (Malkovsky et al., 2012).

Emotion Theory and Boredom

Eastwood et al. (2012) have determined that the bored individual is unaware of his or her own emotions and is externally oriented. They proposed that the underlying problem in boredom might be related to an individual's inability *to access and understand* his or her own emotions (Eastwood et al., 2007). Boredom is associated with limited ability to identify and communicate one's feelings, which also offers suggestions for interventions. Students who have more serious difficulty identifying and describing their own feelings and those of others, may be showing symptoms of alexithymia, and these symptoms are connected to differences in processing negative emotion (Parker, Prkachin, & Prkachin, 2005). When a student is found to have difficulty recognizing and expressing his or her feelings, this is described as alexithymia (Way et al., 2010). Individuals with alexithymia are prone to experience boredom as compare to their peers (Weir, 2013).

Alexithymia is associated with symptom complaints, negative moods, and physical health concerns (Rieffe, Oosterveld, & Terwogt, 2006). Individuals experiencing alexithymia do not analyze situations in a way that helps them identify the causes of their emotions, or helps them deal with their emotions effectively. Alexithymia is a risk factor for a range of problems. The more current understanding of alexithymia is that it relates to a deficit in the processing of emotion (Eastwood et al., 2007).

Alexithymia has been identified in school-aged children as well as in adults. Rieffe et al. (2006) developed an alexithymia questionnaire for children with 20 items representing three factors. The factors include difficulty identifying feelings, difficulty describing feelings, and externally oriented thinking. Children indicate whether or not the item 'is not true,' is 'true,' or is 'a bit true' of them. Difficulty describing and identifying feelings predicts somatic complaints in children. Somatic complaints are more useful for identifying alexithymia in children at the elementary school level as compared to students at the secondary school level. Using the Emotion Awareness Questionnaire, Rieffe and De Rooij (2012) found that the subscale involved with differentiating emotions was a strong predictor of internalizing. The ability to identify emotions and understand what causes them is a feature of alexithymia. Children who do not pay attention to their own emotions and those of others experience depressive feelings and low mood. These children need to understand that emotions give important information that can help them in social situations. The relationship between alexithymia and boredom is clear in that the student who is bored may be unable to access and understand his or her own emotions (Eastwood et al., 2007). This approach to understanding boredom suggests that teaching students to better understand and cope with emotions may be an important component of interventions to increase engagement.

Less Well-Known Theories of Boredom

Several theories involve mental energy: the Menton theory of boredom (Davies & Fortney, 2012) and theories of self-control. Whereas there has been considerable research on the Control-Value Theory of Achievement Emotions, and on attentional and emotion-based theories, the Menton Theory of boredom is purely hypothetical but could have value in deciphering the function of boredom. The theory seems to be somewhat related to the work of Baumeister and colleagues, which does have some support (Baumeister, Bratslavsky, Muraven, & Tice, 1998; Baumeister & Vohs, 2007). The Menton theory is based on units of mental energy (that these theorists call 'mentons'), which are used as an individual engages in various activities. This energy may be attentional, consist of an individual's willpower, or even have to do with glucose, but whatever is eventually determined to be the source of this mental energy, it is allocated to action tasks based on the individual's goals.

In regard to boredom, Davies and Forney's (2012) Menton theory suggests that boredom occurs when there is unused mental energy, or, when there is not enough mental energy. The use of (units of) mental energy can result in feelings of boredom; or, on the other hand, engagement. When the individual does not have sufficient mental energy to engage in a task, such as when the task is too challenging, the individual will experience boredom. Cognitive processing requires mental energy or units of mental energy according to this theory. Tasks that require less cognitive processing require less energy. However, when a task is not challenging enough, the individual will also experience boredom. In this case, the individual has an excess of resources; i.e., more than may be needed for the tasks at hand, so the individual is motivated to find something more interesting. Boredom in this case could have a positive function, supplying motivation for new action to use the surplus energy.

Baumeister et al. (1998) posits that making choices, taking action, and self-regulation draw on this idea of mental energy. Baumeister, Vohs, and Tice (2007) describe a *strength* model of self-control, which suggests that a wide variety of behaviors requiring self-control are driven by a single energy resource. This energy is used for self-control, effortful decision-making, and active responding. Self-control is complex and "biologically expensive" (p. 354). These researchers add that the energy can be depleted. After action is taken using self-control for example, there is a subsequent decrease of energy available for another act of self-control. Baumeister et al. (1998) conducted four students in which the researchers were able to demonstrate depletion of energy following an effort involving self-control.

Inzlicht and Schmeichel (2012) describe what they consider a *resource* model of self-control by describing situations in which there is a temporary depletion of resources in individuals who have utilized self-control to override their response tendencies. A relevant example might be when a student working on a monotonous task is experiencing boredom and yet continues to try to remain on task without success. It could be said that in this example, the student's ability to stay on task will gradually fail as the energy used to stay on task decreases. Inzlicht and Schmeichel indicate that over 100 experiments have been conducted to support the idea of ego depletion.

Self-regulation, effortful choice making, coping with motivation, managing motivational conflict, changing one's behavior to follow rules or match goals, or taking the initiative are volitional acts that use mental energy (Baumeister & Vohs, 2007; Inzlicht & Schmeichel, 2012). After engaging in these activities the individual is temporarily less able and perhaps less willing to engage in another activity, which would require a high degree of self-control. Inzlicht and Schmeichel (2012) recently suggested that exerting self-control could result in motivational and attentional shifts that explain why subsequent self-control would be challenging. Meta-analysis has provided support for the effect of ego depletion on self-control task performance (Hagger, Wood, Stiff, & Chatzisarantis, 2010). Significant effect sizes were found for negatively effecting student effort, perceived challenge or difficulty of tasks, increased negative emotions, tiredness, and decreased blood glucose levels. Dweck and Walton (2010) found that individuals, who believed that their ability to control their emotions and behavior was not limited, did not experience decreased self-control after a laboratory exercise that was designed to deplete their self-control. This suggested that depletion of energy to exert self-control might have to do with beliefs rather than true depletion. All of this research provides additional ideas for intervention. Mental health workers and educators could focus on increasing student motivation (Baumeister & Vohs, 2007), practice self-regulation exercises with students (Gailliot, Plant, Butz, & Baumeister, 2007), provide incentives (Boucher & Kofos, 2012), and/or train self-control.

The Value of Theory

One critical value of the various theories outlined is that they provide ideas for intervention. The ideas for intervention with sufficient support need to be implemented when students are identified as experiencing boredom in school. A group of researchers followed seventh grade students over an entire school year (Ahmed et al., 2013). They found that boredom increased steadily while enjoyment, pride, and math achievement decreased. Researchers suggested that in order to achieve in school, students need the 'skill' to achieve and the 'will' to achieve. These researchers suggested that students also appear to need what they described as the 'thrill' to achieve. The study of boredom in educational settings is new enough, and important enough, to encourage continued and expanding research, and to encourage the interest of educators in recognizing the problem of boredom in the classroom.

Chapter 5
Boredom and Its Relation to Non-cognitive Factors: *Student Motivation, Self-Regulation, Engagement in Learning, and Related Concepts*

Since schools were first established, educators from the inside and reformers from the outside, have tried to change schools for the better. Questions are frequently asked why some students are successful in school while others are not. Why do some students do not complete schooling? Why do some students like school when others do not like school? Why do some students come to school regularly while others stop attending? The popular press may blame the teachers or schools for poor results. Parents may be blamed or accused of not caring. Even students themselves have been blamed for not trying.

Jennings (2012) of the Center on Education Policy describes the major reform movements during the past 50 years and the fact that they have not been entirely successful in improving students' chances to be successful. Add-on services with inadequate funding, school choice, and the test-driven standards movement have all failed to raise the quality of schools according to Jennings. The accountability demands gaining impetus in the 1990s as a critical component of the standards-based reform movement resulted in high-stakes testing. High-stakes testing has been called the "evil twin" (Thompson, 2001, p. 1).

Although there have been some positive effects as a result of reform efforts, they have also been considered stress provoking on students and teachers (Berryhill, Linney, & Fromewick, 2009; Feng, Figlio, & Sass, 2010; Koretz, Barron, Mitchell, & Stecher, 1996; Smith & Rottenberg, 1991; Triplett, Barksdale, & Leftwich, 2003). When the effects of state-mandated testing were compared between several states, at-risk students, students who performed poorly, students at the elementary levels, and students in urban school systems, were impacted more negatively (Clarke et al., 2003). In some cases classes became less responsive to the needs of the students in those classes due to the need to prepare for the important tests.

© Springer International Publishing Switzerland 2015
G.L. Macklem, *Boredom in the Classroom*, SpringerBriefs in Psychology 1,
DOI 10.1007/978-3-319-13120-7_5

Non-cognitive Factors Influencing Student Achievement

Educators have attempted explanations including academic skill deficits and cognitive reasons for lack of student achievement. However, the general public, and even educators themselves have not been keenly aware of the work of scientific researchers and the work that is being done in regard to non-cognitive factors as they influence achievement (Lipnevich & Roberts, 2012; Mega et al., 2013; Shernoff, 2013). Although both Dr. David Wechsler and Dr. Richard Woodcock (McGrew, 2013) recognized the importance of *nonintellectual* factors in school functioning, academic emotions have received little attention in education or in school psychology practice (Valiente et al., 2012). There are a number of non-cognitive factors, which can affect achievement (see Table 5.1).

To complicate matters, the literature surrounding non-cognitive factors in school achievement encompasses research threads from several different areas, resulting in conflicting terms, theories, hypotheses, and conflicting research studies. This makes the body of literature confusing and difficult to organize. In fact, it is challenging to separate academic achievement from motivation, self-regulation, identity, beliefs, goals, and cognition (Berg, 2007).

Table 5.1 Non-cognitive factors influencing academic achievement include

• Attitudes toward school and learning
• Beliefs about the value of education
• Emotions and emotion regulation
• Student goals, student engagement
• Socio-affective skills
• Learning processes
• Dispositions
• Organizational skills
• Academic motivation
• Self-regulation
• Test-taking strategies
• Educational readiness
• Psychosocial characteristics (self-efficacy, self-concept, confidence)
• Conscientiousness
• Metacognitive skills
• Goal orientation
• Time management skills
• Study habits
• Coping strategies
• Attitudes toward different content and subject areas
• Personality factors such as openness and emotional stability

Source: Berg (2007), Goetz et al. (2010), and Lipnevich and Roberts (2012)

Student Engagement

Shernoff (2013) defines student engagement as "the heightened simultaneous experience of concentration, interest, and enjoyment in the task at hand" (p. 12). Engagement is highest during middle childhood while student are still at the elementary level (Mahatmya, Lohman, Matjasko, & Farb, 2012). Engagement drops as students transition from elementary to middle school. A study of high school students found that they were less engaged in school than they were in settings other than public school. They were less interested in what was going in class than in other parts of their lives. Even when concentrating in class, students reported they did not experience enjoyment. They indicated that they thought about the topic of the class only about 60 % of the time. One of the only activities that students felt more negatively about than classwork was homework. Ethnic minority students with strong ethnic identities generally are engaged in school (Bingham & Okagaki, 2012). Low-income Black students report higher levels of engagement and motivation than their peers (Shernoff, 2013). However, having a weak racial identity has been associated with weak engagement in some studies. Students who believe that achievement is appropriate for their group are protected to some degree from the negative influence of discrimination on school achievement. This is especially true for girls. Supportive teachers, sensitive to the challenges of minority students, and acknowledging their strengths, help minority students value schooling.

Engagement is multidimensional and involves emotions, behaviors, and cognitions (Shernoff, 2013). Positive emotions support engagement and coping in the school setting. Emotions influence engagement, which then impacts learning and achievement (Pekrun & Linnenbrink-Garcia, 2012). Most important, emotions have strong effects on attentional engagement with academic tasks. Engagement results in positive outcomes and decreases negative emotions. Conceptually, engagement and self-regulated learning overlap. Engagement predicts learning, grades, and behavior in the short-term (Lam, Wong, Yang, & Lui, 2012). Persistence in adolescence is related to engagement in the school setting (Padilla-Walker, Day, Dyer, & Black, 2013). In the long-term, engagement affects self-esteem. Engagement can be a protective factor against many different negative outcomes.

Many decades of studies have shown that students experience low engagement in the classroom (Marks, 2000). Student engagement decreases as students transition from middle to high school and the gap between engaged and disengaged students continues to increase from eighth to tenth grades (Shernoff, 2013). There is a modest relationship between engagement and achievement. High achieving students with low engagement may achieve in school partly because they find school easy.

There are three dimensions of engagement: behavioral, cognitive, and emotional (Mahatmya et al., 2012). Emotional and cognitive engagement are related to the degree to which students value and connect with classroom activities, and whether or not they believe that the activities are relevant. Motivation is a precursor to each of these. Researchers exploring student engagement use the term *emotional engagement* when studying the feelings and emotions that students experience in learning situations (Shernoff, 2013). Emotional engagement is associated with motivation over time. It provides the incentive to participate behaviorally and to persist (Finn & Zimmer, 2012). Emotional engagement may act indirectly on achievement and effects are inconsistent, although generally positive. Emotional engagement, liking learning, and liking school, has the highest connection with instructional contexts (Lam et al., 2012). When interventions are directed toward emotional engagement they can affect all three types of engagement.

Skinner, Furrer, Marchand, and Kindermann (2008) looked at the emotional engagement of seventh grade students. These researchers determined that emotional engagement was a significant factor in achievement when teacher support was provided to students. Emotional engagement may provide the energy needed for behavioral and cognitive engagement. When students like learning, and like school, Lam et al. (2012) would describe this as being *affectively* engaged. Students in grades 7–10, who experience positive emotions, cope well with academic challenges. Adaptive coping mediates the connection between positive emotions and engagement but only in part. Students, who experience few positive emotions and higher levels of negative emotions, have lower engagement with school and learning. A survey of students who left high school indicated that no single reason was identified to explain dropping out, although 47 % said that a major reason was being bored and disengaged (Bridgeland, Dilulio, & Morison, 2006).

Motivation

Motivation has recently been included in discussions of student engagement (Wolters & Taylor, 2012). Motivation is part of what it is to be a self-regulated learner. Students' beliefs about whether or not they can be successful in school, or self-efficacy, is considered a motivational construct within models of self-regulated learning. Motivation underpins engagement (Martin, 2012). Motivation occurs before the student engages in a task and is part of a task. Motivation and goals occur before cognitive, emotional, and behavioral engagement. Engagement mediates motivation, emotion, and achievement. Motivation that has to do with task involvement is a form of engagement (Pekrun & Linnenbrink-Garcia, 2012). Boredom relates negatively to motivational variables, in the same way as other negative emotions. Boredom undermines motivational engagement. Boredom can result in shallow information processing. Boredom depletes cognitive resources and is generally bad for achievement. Motivation is goal directed (Seo et al., 2004). A major component of motivational theory is goal-setting theory. The idea is that how a person feels when goals are set affects information processing.

Several motivation theories may be relevant to a discussion of boredom in learning environments: these include attribution theory, self-regulated learning, and goals theory. Motivational theories help educators understand emotions in the classroom (Meyer & Turner, 2006). In order to engage students, students need to experience positive emotional experiences. These experiences build a positive classroom climate, which is the basis of student-teacher relationships and interactions. Studies show that students' intrinsic motivation decreases as student go through school and particularly during junior high (Ahmed et al., 2013). Intrinsic motivation can be thought of as a student's enjoyment of learning.

Motivation for success in school can conflict with leisure time activities. School-leisure conflict is associated with decreased concentration in class; hopelessness associated with academics; and, decreased intention to stay in school (Ratelle, Senècal, Vallerand, & Provencher, 2005). Grund, Brassier, and Fries (2014) examined the conflict between a desire to study and desire to engage in leisure activities. Even when students decided to study, simply knowing that there are alternatives can affect their work, and negatively affect the students' self-regulation. The more intense their interest in the conflicting leisure activity, the less persistent students may be, and the more difficult it may be to concentrate when studying. There is apparently a *motivational interference effect* that affects self-regulation. Grund and colleagues were able to demonstrate this interference effect on enjoyment and success both academically and socially.

Interests

Interest is component of motivation. Interests are affective states that involve feelings of arousal, alertness, attention, and concentration (Ainley, 2006; Berg, 2007). Interests are preceded by dispositions, and are affected by consequences. Interests are a key variable in motivation and may connect achievement goals to engagement. Ainley (2006) thinks of interest as an emotional state representing the subjective experience of learning. Interest may represent the integration of emotion, motivation, and cognition. Prior interests and goals are focused on the task at hand as interest and motivation come together. The concept of interest is considered a subset of emotional engagement, with motivation a subset of cognitive engagement (Ainley, 2012). This is a good example of the complexity and intertwining nature of the various concepts.

Research on student interests indicates that students who start a semester with moderate or high interest in a class or subject area maintain that level of interest. Students, who initially react to course content with low interest, stay at that low level of interest (Ainley, 2010). Students who begin a course in school with little interest in the subject, and who do not have their interest improved by the teacher, or materials, or content, are not likely to become engaged.

Lack of interest can cause boredom but interest and boredom are not the same (Pekrun et al., 2010). Boredom is more painful than interest, and boredom triggers a desire to escape from the situation. Boredom, but not interest, results in avoidance motivation.

Beliefs, Attributions, and Appraisals

Weiner (1985) proposed that one's beliefs about whether or not she/he will succeed or fail, along with the individual's emotions, guide motivated behavior. This *attributional theory* addresses both motivation and emotion. Students' perceived reasons for success and failure influence achievement. When these perceptions are stable, the students' expectations to be successful are influenced positively or negatively. Expectancy and emotions in turn influence behavior and motivation.

Blackwell, Trzesniewski, and Dweck (2007) conducted two studies with seventh grade students to investigate students' theories of intelligence. Students who believed that intelligence was malleable also had stronger learning goals, believed that effort would make a difference, and exhibited fewer 'helpless' attributions. When faced with possible failure, these students chose effort-based approaches and as a result they achieved at a higher rate over the middle school transition. In addition they increased math grades over the next several years.

Appraisal theories of emotion indicate that hopelessness and helplessness have both affective and cognitive components (Daniels et al., 2009). Hopelessness and helplessness occur as a reaction of student appraisals of control and stability. When students feel that they are in control in regard to their goals, they feel hopeful. Hopefulness has been shown to predict positive outcomes including graduation from high school. When students feel that their goals cannot be reached and they are therefore no longer in control, they may feel helpless. Students who feel helpless find it difficult to act. They react passively and may experience symptoms of depression.

Boredom reduces motivation, attention, and processing of information because it is a deactivating emotion. It has this effect by influencing underlying appraisals (Daniels et al., 2009). In this way it lowers achievement. Interestingly, Daniels et al. speculate that the emotional consequences of boring experiences may continue on after the present activity has been completed. This is important information for educators and emphasizes the importance of recognizing and dealing with boredom to the extent possible, as soon as it is recognized.

Goals

Theorists and researchers who focus on motivation have suggested that the classroom environment is key to goal formation (Seifert, 1997). Seifert argued that emotions are critical for goal formation as well. In a study involving tenth grade students in Newfoundland and Labrador, groups of students, with different profiles of emotions, set different goals for themselves. This demonstrates that emotions are tied to goal orientation. Success and failure can impact goal adoption as well.

Achievement goals include mastery goals, performance approach goals, and performance avoidance goals (Pekrun et al., 2009). Mastery goals predict the positive emotions of enjoyment, hope, and pride. Performance-approach goals predict pride. Performance-avoidance goals predict anxiety, hopelessness, and shame. Students who embrace mastery goals consider the feedback they receive related to the effort that they put into the task (Daniels et al., 2009). Achievement goals effect emotions by influencing underlying control and value appraisals. Students who have performance goals tend to interpret the feedback that they receive as an attack on their ability, triggering anxiety. Anxiety, unlike boredom, is predicted by performance goals. Mastery goals have been determined to predict activity emotions (Pekrun et al., 2011).

Mastery goals relate to interest in learning new skills. Performance goals are associated with avoiding negative feedback about one's ability (Furner & Gonzalez-DeHass, 2011). Mastery goals influence student persistence and motivation. Performance goals may push a student toward avoiding challenging tasks. Additionally, there appear to be two types of performance goals. One type involves *approach*, which may stimulate students to compete and do better than their peers. The other approach involves *avoidance* of failure. Performance-avoidance goals interfere with learning and are connected with anxiety. In like manner, there appear to be two types of mastery goals. Mastery *approach* goals are aimed at increasing learning. Mastery *avoidance* goals are found in students who feel they are not competent and fear that they may fail when attempting a task.

In a study with college-age students, Daniels et al. (2009) found hopefulness predicted both mastery and performance goals. Helplessness on the other hand interfered with the development of mastery goals. Mastery goals led to enjoyment. Boredom and anxiety interfered with the development of mastery goals across cultures. Task goals are mastery-approach goals (Mouratidis, Vansteenkiste, & Lens, 2009). Relationships between boredom and task goals have been found in for high school students who participated in physical education classes. Students who lack goals and perceive a particular subject as useless are more likely to experience boredom (Daschmann et al., 2011).

Self-Concept

Self-concept is usually considered to be a trait (Goetz et al., 2010). The strength of a student's self-concept and emotion relations seems to be influenced by the subject area, grade level, and emotion type. Self-concept and self-efficacy are overlapping constructs. Academic emotions are expected to have the same relationship with self-concept as with self-efficacy. Academic self-concepts have to do with beliefs in regard to the students' perceptions of control over their learning. Academic self-concept has to do with knowledge and perceptions of oneself in various subjects. Academic self-efficacy has to do with the belief that one can be successful in a given subject area. Self-efficacy beliefs effect thinking, actions, and emotions in a direct manner.

Studies show a strong relationship between academic self-concepts and emotions in students (Goetz et al., 2010). The age of the student, the subject area and the specific emotion in question all make a difference and contribute to variability. Relations between interest, positive emotions, and self-concept grow stronger from grades 1 to 5. Boredom has a somewhat weak relationship with a student's academic self-concept, while enjoyment, anxiety, and anger have stronger relationships. Pride has the strongest relationship with a student's academic self-concept.

Self-Regulated Learning

Self-regulated learning is a key feature of engagement (Wolters & Taylor, 2012). Self-regulated learning has to do with *management* of motivation, behavior, and cognition in the school setting. Self-regulated learning has four phases: planning, monitoring, control or management, and reflection/reaction. Students set goals and then monitor, regulate, and control their learning to reach the goals. Self-regulation has to do with planning, persistence, and thinking about one's actions (Grund et al., 2014). Self-regulated students work hard in class and work hard when studying or doing homework. They choose learning strategies that work, and continue to use them even when the situation is challenging. They are able to adapt or change strategies when they aren't working. The negative aspects of self-regulated learning involve defensive pessimism and self-handicapping, which are considered lapses in self-regulation (Wolters & Taylor, 2012, p. 643).

Emotional processing is a major form of engagement (Wolters & Taylor, 2012). Emotions demand regulation (Ahmed et al., 2013). Emotions drive students to use information-processing strategies. Boredom, as an emotion that decreases arousal, would decrease the likelihood that the student would use learning strategies, particularly meta-cognitive strategies or strategies requiring effort, such as elaboration or critical thinking. Negative emotions can interfere with self-regulation of cognition and also with processing capacity. Effortful processing is decreased in the presence of negative emotions. Ahmed and colleagues demonstrated that initial levels of boredom in a seventh grade student population predicted lower use of meta-cognitive strategies in the classroom. The strategies considered in this study, included rehearsal, elaboration, planning, evaluation, and organizational strategies. Emotions in the classroom are critical for sustaining self-regulated learning. As positive emotions decreased in students, motivation decreased. Boredom showed a steady increase over the school year for these seventh graders.

The Ahmed et al. (2013) study determined that positive emotions among students at this age had greater effects on information-processing strategies than the negative effects of negative emotions. They hypothesized that positive emotions could possibly override the effects of negative emotions on self-regulated learning. This finding is important for practitioners designing interventions to be used by classroom teachers or for assisting small groups of students.

Emotions, self-regulated learning, and motivation are linked (Mega et al., 2013). Mega and colleagues combined three questionnaires, one dealing with self-regulation, one dealing with motivation, and one dealing with emotions, into a single tool. This tool, the Self-Regulated Learning, Emotions, and Motivation Computerized Battery (LEM-B), was studied in an undergraduate student population. Researchers concluded that self-regulation and motivation mediate how emotions effect achievement. Positive emotions allowed students to organize their academic study time and to summarize material making it personally meaningful. Positive emotions effect students' perception of themselves as competent and able to achieve and be successful. Positive emotions alone are not enough however, they must be accompanied by motivation and self-regulated learning.

Chapter 6
Interventions for Externally Triggered Boredom: *So What Can Teachers Do to Add a Bit of Excitement to Learning in the Classroom?*

School professionals are beginning to learn that boredom is related to a wide variety of negative outcomes. Although changing internal causes of boredom may be extremely difficult, identifying the external antecedents of boredom may be manageable. In fact, identifying students who experience *boredom proneness* may be *preventive* and reduce school dropout (Dahlen et al., 2005). We need to proactively address boredom that is being experienced in the K-12 student population, as well as boredom in the university and college-aged populations.

Preventing School Dropout by Addressing Boredom

Engagement is a complex construct (Wu, Anderson, Nguyen-Johiel, & Miller, 2013). Behavioral engagement has to do with participation in tasks. Emotional engagement has to do with the various emotions experienced while participating in classwork. Cognitive engagement is related to investment in thinking and learning. The three types are most likely interrelated. Student engagement can be measured using a tool such as the Student Engagement Instrument (SEI; Appleton, Christenson, Kim, & Reschly, 2006). The self-report tool measures cognitive and psychological engagement. A longitudinal study of ninth grade students using a brief form of the instrument determined that this shorter form could be successfully used to monitor at-risk students in danger of dropping out of school (Pinzone, Appleton, & Reschly, 2014). An understanding of student engagement and disengagement is considered to be critical for understanding school dropout (Christenson, Reschly, & Wylie, 2012).

Educators in K-12 public schools are acutely aware of problems in regard to school dropout. Educational reformers have collected considerable data. In a series of three reports, researchers pointed out that there is no single reason that students drop out of high school (Bridgeland et al., 2006). The process takes place gradually over time rather than being a single event. High school dropout has been labeled an

© Springer International Publishing Switzerland 2015
G.L. Macklem, *Boredom in the Classroom*, SpringerBriefs in Psychology 1,
DOI 10.1007/978-3-319-13120-7_6

epidemic (Bridgeland et al., 2006, p. i). Almost one third of students in public schools drop out in the U.S. Almost half of all black, Hispanic, and Native American students drop out. Of those who dropped out, 47 % of students reported that their classes were not interesting. They shared that they were bored and disengaged when in school. Sixty-nine percent said they were not at all motivated. Student boredom appears to be a major variable in school drop out and there is some concern that boredom is increasing among student populations (Belton & Priyadharshini, 2007). Boredom is sometimes blamed on the school. At other times it is blamed on students (Larson & Richards, 1991), or on parents (Bridgeland, Dilulio, & Balfanz, 2009). Blaming does not solve problems and may even prevent some problems from being addressed.

Educators seem to blame parents for the high school dropout problem as researchers discovered in the second of the three reports (Bridgeland et al., 2009). Sixty-one percent of teachers and 45 % of principals cited a lack of support at home as a factor in most incidences of school dropout. Twenty percent of teachers, and 21 % of principals, felt that boredom was involved. This conflicts with survey reports in which students who dropped out of high school reported that they found classes boring and not relevant. The educators who felt that boredom was involved, also felt if students complained of boredom, they were just making excuses.

In the third report, researchers repeated their findings about the conflicting views of educators and students about the reasons for school drop out (Bridgeland, Balfanz, Moore, & Friant, 2010). According to the third report, the number one reason for dropping out of school, as reported by students, was their inability to see connections between schooling and their own lives. Students considered the skills taught in school *unusable* and they felt disengaged. For this third report researchers brought students, parents, and teachers together from cities in Maryland, Texas, Indiana, and Tennessee to participate in focus groups. The report serves as a model for bringing people together and moving beyond the 'blame game,' with the goal of making courses more interesting and relevant. They also demonstrated the need to involve parents, and the need to provide supports for each group of stakeholders in order to keep students in school.

The research on school dropout has focused on the transition from grade 8 to 9 in the past, given that school dropout starts early, and antecedents continue to increase the pressure to drop out of school over time (Bowers & Sprott, 2012). A recent study examined students who dropped out after grade 10. This study identified three different groups of dropouts. The students in these three groups expressed different feelings about school and different observations of their experiences in grade 10. The three groups appeared to have needed different intervention strategies in order to stay in school. Quiet students who dropped out would have benefitted from tutoring and closer connections to school in order to reduce absences and failure. Jaded students would have needed positive ways to connect with school because their views were so negative. Involved students would have needed flexible schedules and alternative paths toward graduation.

At the high school level, Gregory, Allen, Mikami, Hafen, and Pianta (2014) speculate that teachers may be more interested in changing the instructional climate than the emotional climate in the classroom. In urban high schools, researchers conducting studies on cutting classes, found that students cutting classes claimed that they were bored in school. The concerns around student boredom need to be taken seriously by educators (Bowers & Sprott, 2012).

As ways to reduce boredom in K-12 schools begins to be explored, it is important to recognize that this may not be an easy task. Researchers working on expanding our knowledge of academic emotions in general, and boredom in particular, acknowledge that it is not likely that boredom could truly be totally prevented (Pekrun et al., 2010). Some students may experience boredom even when they have the chance to be placed in high quality classrooms (Daschmann et al., 2011). For example, computer-based learning environments are often motivating for students. In a study involving computer-based learning involving different populations, different measures, and games versus two tutoring systems, researchers examined the incidence, persistence, and impact of boredom and other achievement emotions (Baker et al., 2010). The most common emotions experienced by students were engaged concentration (most common) and confusion (second most common). In the interactive learning environment, boredom was associated with 'gaming the system.' Gaming the system refers to guessing systematically without learning the material. Boredom was considered by the study authors more critical to attend to than student frustration. Frustration is part of the processing of information for learning, but boredom is not. Boredom was persistent in the several learning environments, more persistent than any other emotion. Frustration was less persistent. In fact, boredom was the most persistent emotion and acted as if it were a non-transitory mood. Researchers concluded:

> Once a student is bored, it appears to be difficult to transition out of boredom—suggesting that it is important to prevent boredom before it ever occurs (Baker et al., 2010, p. 19).

The study suggested that boredom should be detected and responded to quickly in interactive learning environments, in that boredom can interfere with learning. If we accept the fact that there are multiple causes of boredom in students, and that these might be categorized in a simplistic manner; that is, boredom caused by the environment as apposed to boredom stemming from the student, it may be easier to begin to explore interventions. Clearly environments are easier to change than personality traits.

Reducing Boredom in the School Environment

Schutz and Lanehart (2002) assert: "Emotions are intimately involved in virtually every aspect of the teaching and learning process and, therefore, an understanding of the nature of emotions within the school context is essential" (p. 67). When addressing the causes of boredom in the school environment, it is important to look carefully at the types of tasks presented, the environment, the individual student, and the student-environment fit (Fisherl, 1993). This is important for all learning environments at all levels of education.

Numerous aspects of instruction are involved in generating boredom in students (Daschmann et al., 2011). These include the quality of classroom instruction, although quality of classroom instruction is also influenced by students' feelings of control and value beliefs. Prevention of over-challenge is important in classroom situations as is providing students feedback to highlight growth, rather than inducing discouragement (Goetz et al., 2010). Improving clarity of instruction, structure of delivery, and engaging students in cognitively activating tasks, should increase a student's sense of control over their own learning, and also help the student value the content more (Pekrun, 2006). Assigning authentic tasks will reduce boredom. Tasks must also give students a chance to master them. Matching the task to student's capability can increase the value of the tasks for the student, and make the tasks more enjoyable.

Teachers who present challenging material that is not beyond the capacity of any student in the class, would reduce boredom in the classroom as difficult as that may be (Pekrun et al., 2010). One approach that teachers have used when their classes are quite diverse is to adjust instruction toward the middle ability or competency levels of the class. This approach unfortunately could induce boredom in some of the students (Daschmann et al., 2011).

Teacher Behavior

Teachers are the adults who most directly impact students' boredom (Daschmann, 2013). In fact there is clear evidence of a relationship between teacher's behavior and students' engagement (Skinner & Belmont, 1993). Teachers' interactions with students predict students' behavioral and emotional engagement. Students know when their teacher likes them. When teachers are extremely controlling, giving frequent directives, not allowing any comments that might be construed as critical or independent, and interfere with students' learning pace, even fourth and fifth grade children experience anxiety or anger as demonstrated in a study in Israel (Assor, Kaplan, Kanat-Maymon, & Roth, 2005). In classrooms with a controlling teacher, motivation decreases. Positive student-teacher relationships; i.e. when teachers learn about students so that they feel that the teacher knows them, can significantly impact student engagement (Gregory et al., 2014).

Classroom teachers can create environments that can influence whether or not boredom occurs. Focusing on increasing how students think about the content of courses so that they perceive that the content is more valuable to them, or more interesting to them, would be an important way to reduce boredom in the classroom (Pekrun et al., 2010). Teacher enthusiasm has been connected to the development of values in the classroom (Frenzel, Pekrun, & Goetz, 2007). When teachers talk about academic values with their students this makes a difference in a classroom situation and effects the development of a sense of value in the content (Pekrun, 2006).

The actual learning tasks assigned in class need to have value for students and they need to meet students' needs. Enthusiasm can be communicated through emotional contagion and students' value of the activities may be enhanced. Instructions make a difference when students are working on tasks. Sawin and Scerbo (1995) instructed students to be vigilant or instructed students to relax when working on vigilance tasks. Students with low boredom proneness outperformed those with high boredom proneness. They also reported less boredom in completing the tasks. Students additionally need some autonomy in learning situations (Pekrun, 2006).

Teachers can make a difference in decreasing boredom in school among students at all levels of the educational system; the elementary, middle, and high school levels. High ability students in the fifth to ninth grades have been found to experience considerable boredom when they felt that they were not being challenged or stimulated (Mora, 2011). Repetitive activities are related to boredom. Disengaged students in middle and early high school associate classroom practices with boredom more than content or subject matter. Middle school students prefer learning skills rather than dealing with abstract content. They respond better to demonstrations than book-driven material.

When high school students were asked about types of class work that engaged them on the High School Survey of Student Engagement Survey (HSSE) (http://ceep.indiana.edu), 61 % rated discussion and debate as engaging, and 60 % rated group projects engaging. Students positively rated student presentations, engaging in role-plays, discussion and debate, assignments that involved art and drama, and projects in which they could use technology (Yazzie-Mintz, 2010). The traditional approach to instruction in the classroom is teacher-centered with lectures (Muis & Duffy, 2013) and this may need to change somewhat. Daschmann, Goetz, and Stupnisky (2014) found that the cause of boredom most commonly identified by students had to do with the characteristics of instruction.

Researchers have found that boredom is associated with student beliefs that the classroom content has no personal value for a given student. If teachers used strategies that explain and reinforce the value of achievement, this approach might be very helpful in decreasing boredom. Associating learning with positive outcomes might add meaning to the task of learning (Nett et al., 2011). Teachers dealing with the goals of NCLB high stakes testing, and also dealing with keeping students engaged have considerable challenge. Situated boredom can occur in classes that prepare students for high stakes tests (Mora, 2011). Low achieving students have higher affective needs (Woolf et al., 2010). Even having knowledge of the importance of students' affective needs, it is difficult to provide interventions that have a profound effect on students' emotions (Efklides & Volet, 2005).

In class, the student who frequently perceives teacher punishment, experiences more frequent feelings of boredom (Frenzel et al., 2007). Researchers recommend that teachers increase the structure of the classroom environment, keep track of student's comprehension, talk about academic values, teach enthusiastically, provide incentives for task completion and good behavior, and engage all of the students in a class to decrease perceptions of boredom. Teachers also need to appreciate the fact that students who complain may not be motivated to attack the teacher but rather may be expressing their own inability to engage in the lesson (Nett et al., 2011). No matter how hard a teacher may try, a particular student may still perceive a class a boring. Teachers who can learn (with the help of a school psychologist) to reframe student complaints and mild misbehavior with difficulties in attention may be able to respond to individual students in more helpful ways. Teachers might have their students make 'benefit lists' of how course content may have value for them. An activity like this might help students increase their perceived value of the course and its content as students share their lists with one another.

Offering Choices

Giving students choices has been associated with strategies that teachers can use to decrease boredom (Caldwell, Darling, Payne, & Dowdy, 1999). Students may feel more in control, more motivated, and more positive when they are given choices (Patall, 2013). Choices of whom they work with, and group projects can help students make connections between the material and its applications (Gregory et al., 2014). Current research suggests that giving students a choice in regard to some aspects of a task works well when students already have some interest in the task. Motivated students who are already interested in the activity (assignment) benefit more than poorly motivated students when given an opportunity to make choices. The requirement to make a choice becomes an additional burden for poorly motivated students who experience 'choice' as an additional stressor when they already don't enjoy the task. However for students initially interested in a given task, when these students are asked to repeat a task, being given a choice makes them more willing to work on tasks that are not engaging. Choice does not help when the task is perceived as uninteresting from the beginning. Unfortunately, a number of factors influence whether giving students a choice is helpful or not.

Encouraging Mastery Goals

Goal structures can be individualistic, competitive, or cooperative (Pekrun, 2006). In an individualistic goal structure environment, achievement has to do with mastery of the material. In competitive situations, achievement depends on the group and involves performance goals. In cooperative situations, goals are linked to peer interactions.

Because different goal structures provide different chances of success, they will affect students' perceived control. The three different structures have different effects on students' feelings of control and will affect students of different abilities differently. In classes in which social comparison standards are prevalent, some students will have negative experiences. Expectations should not be beyond the capability of a student.

When teachers emphasize mastery goals, and stress the importance of hard work so that students grow, improve, and learn, students will be more likely to exhibit positive motivation (Furner & Gonzalez-DeHass, 2011). An emphasis on mastery approach goals encourages on-task behavior and discourages off-task behaviors and anxiety. A mastery-oriented classroom would connect lessons and activities to the 'real world' by providing authentic tasks connected to students' interests. Activity would be interactive so that all students were involved. Cooperative activities would be provided so students could collaborate on tasks. Teachers would help students understand how to use self-regulated strategies like goal setting and self-assessment. Students would have some choice in regard to the focus of their assignments or in regard to their final projects. Students would be encouraged to strive for their personal best. Finally the classroom climate would allow for risk-taking, question asking, and an understanding that errors are part of the learning process.

Schools certainly need to encourage the adoption of mastery goals. However, in addition, it is necessary to integrate achievement goals with a focus on achievement *emotions* such as boredom (Pekrun et al., 2009). Teachers also need to be careful about too much focus on goals, as this could interfere with enjoying coursework or learning (Turner & Husman, 2008). Good teaching requires a delicate balance of talking about goals while conveying enthusiasm about the content at hand.

Molding Student Appraisals

Appraisal theory such as the control-value theory, suggests that teachers can change student's emotions directly by addressing appraisals (Pekrun, 2006). The way in which an individual student thinks about his or her intelligence is connected to how the student *feels* in school (King, McInerney, & Watkins, 2012). Students who think that intelligence is fixed and cannot change, experience more boredom and other negative emotions in class. Feedback from the teacher can determine students' appraisals of achievement, and in this way effect students' emotional reactions (Pekrun, 2006). Teachers need to teach students that failure represents an opportunity to learn.

Blackwell et al. (2007) found that the belief that intelligence can be changed predicted increasing grades over the 2 years of junior high school. Students who believed that intelligence was fixed and unchangeable, did not improve grades. An intervention designed to change the thinking of seventh grade students who believed intelligence was fixed positively affected student motivation. Three times as many students who learned intelligence was malleable, increased effort and school engagement as compared with a control group. The students with the fixed beliefs (entity theory as opposed to incremental theory) evidenced decreasing grades.

Teachers must try to change a student's beliefs about his/her own competencies in specific subject areas (Goetz et al., 2010), by helping students see that improvement has to do with their competency in that particular content area. This would increase sense of control in regard to academic progress and improve students' academic self-concepts. It is important that this be done in *each* separate content area rather than in general due to domain specificity. Academic emotions, sense of control, and feelings of competence are different depending on the given subject. Relations between academic self-concept and emotions also depend on the age of students and the particular subject or content area. For high school students, improving a student's self-concepts may decrease negative emotions.

Active Learning

Mora (2011) concluded that more interactive hands-on activities resulted in decreased boredom among students in the classroom. There has been a considerable amount of research to support the idea that active or interactive teaching strategies are more effective than didactic methods (Macklem, 2014, pp. 55–57). Students rate interactive approaches highly. Prevention programs in particular have found more success when learning was interactive; non-interactive programming was not found to be as effective.

Active learning is student-centered (Smith & Cardaciotto, 2011). Students become engaged in doing something meaningful and thinking about it. Active learning positively effects student' attitudes, motivation, memory, and test scores. Prince (2004) defined active learning "as any instructional method that engages students in the learning process" (p. 223). A student engaged in active learning would be involved in meaningful activities and would be thinking about what he or she were doing. The key elements of active learning are student activity and engagement.

Interactive learning includes the use of small group discussions, brainstorming, debates, write-pair-share activities, role-play, collaborative learning, cooperative learning, games, etc. (Farrell, 2009; Prince, 2004). Prince (2004) found all forms of active learning effective. Teaching strategies that would be considered to foster active learning have several commonalities: students are doing something rather than simply listening; the goal is skill development as opposed to information gathering; thinking skills are involved; students are engaged in an activity; and students attitudes and values are a focus (Bonwell & Eison, 1991; Farrell, 2009). Active learning shows improved gains in learning, greater conceptual understanding of basic concepts, positive student attitudes, improved skill development, and better recall.

Michael (2006) felt that active learning instructional practices were supported by evidence from different disciplines. Studies indicate that active learning improves the achievement of minorities and the lowest-performing children in the class (Johnson, Johnson, & Holubec, 1992). A study of seventh grade students in Turkey demonstrated that problem-based active leaning improved students' achievement and attitudes in science classes. A meta-analysis of 207 school-based drug prevention programs determined that interactive programs had greater effects than lecture-oriented programs (Tobler et al., 2000).

An interesting study by Wu et al. (2013) compared students' motivation and academic motivation during small group discussions versus whole class discussion.

They compared 6-min periods of collaborative, peer-led discussions with 6-min whole class discussions in classes of fourth and fifth graders. They provided evidence to indicate that collaborative discussions were helpful for increasing motivation. The small group discussions with minimal teacher involvement were stimulating for students. They appreciated the freedom of choice and ability to control turn taking and the topic. The study also found that this approach was particularly helpful for lower ability students. Girls reported more interest and engagement than boys in both types of discussion models. Boys preferred the collaborative discussions and found them interesting.

Decreasing Distractions to Prevent Boredom

Early on, researchers connected being distracted to boredom in the classroom (Damrad-Frye & Laird, 1989). These researchers found that students felt bored while working on a task when a distracting noise was presented at even quite low levels. This type of distraction affected introverts more than extroverts but interestingly the students tended to blame the course material rather than the distraction. Reducing distractions in the classroom may be important. Reducing distractions might be even more important when students are studying although this has not as yet been explored.

Students' Perceptions of Boredom in the Classroom

If educators want to reduce boredom in the classroom, they need to be able to identify what it is about the classroom that students perceive as boring (Vogel-Walcutt et al., 2012). Daschmann (2013) administered an open-ended questionnaire to ninth grade students to determine what they thought caused boredom in the classroom. Teachers were interviewed to determine their perceptions as well. Both students and teachers identified the causes of boredom typically found in the literature. A subset of parents were administered a questionnaire as well. Parents were found to have a good understanding of their child's boredom in regard to frequency and intensity. Most students felt that boredom they experienced in class had to do with the instruction. They described characteristics of teacher instruction such as talking too long, or too many writing tasks, as boring. Teachers focused more on students being over challenged or under challenged. Researchers noted that even though teachers were aware of what would be perceived as boring by students, they concluded that it is apparently very difficult for teachers to avoid boredom.

The Precursors to Boredom Scale developed by Daschmann et al. (2011) identifies a variety of situations, setting, activities, that contribute to student boredom. Research on this scale was conducted with German students in grade 5–10. The scale is specific to math classes in that boredom is context and subject specific.

Students responded using a 5-point Likert scale. The goal was to let teachers know what was causing students in their class to experience boredom. Mean scores might help teachers adapt instructional approaches. The tool addresses eight different possible antecedents of boredom: monotony; lack of meaning; opportunity costs (which refers to whether or not a students would rather engage in other activities); being over-challenged; a lack of involvement (not feeling that one is integrated in class interaction); teacher dislike; and generalized boredom (a habitual feeling or dispositional boredom). This tool needs to be standardized on a large sample. The knowledge of what may be causing boredom in the environment or between the individual students and the environment will be critical for prevention.

When students engage in interactive activities in the classroom, teachers need to detect boredom quickly and respond immediately. When teachers can identify what is causing boredom in their classroom, they will be able to adapt instructional strategies so that they can reduce boredom (Daschmann et al., 2014) (see Table 6.1).

Helping Students Process Emotions in the Classroom

Emotional awareness can predict differences in boredom among students (Eastwood et al., 2007). A student who is bored may not be aware of his or her emotions. Advocating and assisting with the implementation of an evidence-based, social-emotional learning curricula in the general classroom can address the development of competent emotional development. School psychologists can provide schools with consultation to implement universal social emotional learning curricula that directly teaches emotion vocabulary, emotional awareness, and emotion regulation skills.

The ability to use a feelings vocabulary is considered to be one of the key skills of emotional competence (Beck, Kumschick, Eid, & Klann-Delius, 2012). Researchers investigating the relationships between various components of language competency and emotional competency have determined that receptive vocabulary and literacy are closely related to emotional awareness and knowledge. This is the case not only for the early childhood period but also for children in the 7–9 year range. In fact, connecting words to specific emotions and feelings have positive effects throughout one's life (Izard, 2009). Learning new emotion words encourages the development of emotional abilities related to understanding others. Putting feelings into words facilitates emotion regulation and high-level social skills. Students who are able to use emotion vocabulary are more socially efficacious as compared to their peers. Emotion words provide the context for emotion perception, which explains why children with semantic deficits have weaknesses in emotion perception (Gendron, Lindquist, Barsalou, & Barrett, 2012).

Schonert-Reichl and Lawlor (2010) evaluated the effects of a mindfulness education program in which students in the fourth to seventh grades engaged in mindful attention training three times a day. This universal prevention intervention consisted of ten manualized lessons of mindful practices or training exercises. Lessons

Table 6.1 Recommendations for reducing externally generated boredom from the literature

Changing adults	Changing instruction	Changing tasks	Changing the environment
Appreciating that instruction can be perceived as boring	Matching material to student ability	Design cognitively activating tasks for students	Addressing student absence as possibly related to boredom or lack of meaning
Addressing student connections with the school	Improve the clarity of instruction	Design authentic tasks connected to student interests	Identify student strengths and believe in students' ability to achieve
Learn something about each student	Giving students more control over their own learning	Include or increase classroom discussions	Develop a team of professionals to select an evidence-based social-emotional learning curriculum to implement in the general education program
Talk about academic values with students (the value of achievement, positive outcomes of schooling, importance of hard work)	Allow independent (even critical) comments and provide an appropriate level of autonomy	Utilize group projects, role-plays, art, drama, small group discussions, games, and debates	
Attend to student affective needs	Consider pacing of instruction	Provide interactive and cooperative activities	
Pay attention when students appear or report being bored	Deliver lessons enthusiastically		
Partner with the school psychologist to implement a values-affirmation intervention with fidelity	Include demonstrations		
	Provide incentives for tasks completion and appropriate behavior		
	Offer choices regarding with whom to work and around group projects for students who are interested		
	Match structure to student needs		
	Teach students goal setting and self-assessment		
	Teach students that failure provides an opportunity to learn		
	Teach an 'emotions' vocabulary		

included learning about affirmations, how to eliminate negative thinking, acknowledging one another, making friends, and teamwork. Significant improvements in social and emotional competence, improved attention and concentration, improved self-concepts, and increased positive emotions were noted. The program worked better for preadolescents than early adolescents. Schonert-Reichl et al. (2011) conducted a study with fourth and fifth graders randomly assigned to receive the MindUp curriculum by the Hawn Foundation (http://thehawnfoundation.org). Children who participated evidenced improvements in cognitive control, regulation of stress, decreased negative emotions, increased positive emotions, and improved math grades.

Given researchers feel that boredom may be related to being out of touch with one's emotions, universal and targeted training in emotional awareness may be in order (Eastwood et al., 2007). Students who experience boredom have been found to have difficulty identifying their emotions. It would be important for these students to participate in a specific social-emotional learning curriculum that emphasizes training in identifying emotions in ones' self and others, and to learn to develop and connect emotion vocabulary to the emotions that the student perceives.

Social-emotional learning (SEL) programs for preschool, and also for grades K-5, have been investigated by the Center for Social and Emotional Learning (CASEL) (http://www.casel.org/guide/ratings/elementary). A number of strong programs for schools include at least some direct instruction in emotions. One example of a curriculum that specifically addresses learning about emotions is the *RULER Feeling Words Curriculum* developed by the Yale Center for Emotional Intelligence (Brackett, Rivers, Reyes, & Salovey, 2012). Students participating in this curriculum exhibited better work habits, improved social development, and higher academic performance in English language arts.

School psychologists can assist schools in locating, evaluating, and implementing additional curricula that focuses on emotions, that are age appropriate, and that fit a given school. SEL curricula benefit all children. A meta-analysis (SEL Research Group/CASEL, 2010) comparing students in SEL programs delivered in the school setting to students who do not participate included:

- improved social and emotional skills;
- improved attitudes about themselves and their peers;
- better social behavior and behavior in class, with reduced misbehavior and aggression;
- reduced emotional stress and depressive symptoms; and
- an 11-point gain in academic achievement.

In a randomized controlled trial of the *Responsive Classroom*, researchers found that second through fifth grade students determined that social-emotional learning did not interfere with academic achievement in students (Rimm-Kaufman et al., 2014). The responsive classroom approach positively influenced student-teacher relationships, and supported self-control, which in turn influenced achievement. Students with low initial math achievement benefitted most.

No matter which of the strongest SEL curricula best fits a given school, achievement gains are a strong selling point for teachers and administrators. Importantly, SEL programming delivered by teachers has been demonstrated to be effective. Personnel from outside the school are not needed to deliver the curriculum in order to get positive results (SEL Research Group/CASEL, 2010). However, curricula that directly instructs students in emotional processing would be most applicable for teachers who want to reduce boredom in their classrooms.

Chapter 7
Interventions for Internal Variables: *Some Students Just Can't Turn It On—They Will Need More than Great Teachers and Interesting Lessons*

Boredom, as an emotion, seems simple; but it is, in fact, very complex (Fahlman, Mercer, Gaskovski, Eastwood, & Eastwood, 2009). Eastwood et al. (2007) argue that boredom "ought to be a more central focus of psychological inquiry" (p. 1043). Along with research interest, school-based mental health workers must begin to address this emotion among the student population for whom boredom is chronic, internally generated, or is easily induced in environments that may be stimulating for others but are not for the students in this group.

There are several ways in which mental health professions in K-12 schools and in colleges can service students and the teachers with whom they collaborate, in relation to student boredom. A first step would involve sharing the prevalence of boredom among students with teachers, and suggesting ways of increasing engagement as part of individual teacher consultation, team consultation (grade level meetings), or Inservice education for teachers. These services could be introduced around preventing school dropout, preventing disengagement or increasing engagement, and/or addressing student effort and motivation.

The same students, who report being bored frequently while engaged in schoolwork, also report being bored during non-school activities. For non-school activities, helping adolescents make better choices of activities, decreasing adult control of the activity, and adding structure, may reduce boredom. In addition, reducing students' felt pressure to engage in particular activities may reduce feelings of boredom (Caldwell et al., 1999; Shaw, Caldwell, & Kleiber, 1996). Girls particularly benefit from reduced stress of participation to please others. School-based mental health professionals may be helpful in sharing this information with parents and school personnel involved in non-academic school activities.

Beyond this beginning, mental health professionals can service students with high boredom proneness in a variety of ways depending on whether the student issues have to do with finding meaning in life, having difficulties with attentional regulation, having negative appraisals of their ability, lacking emotional awareness, or experiencing deficits in self-regulation.

© Springer International Publishing Switzerland 2015
G.L. Macklem, *Boredom in the Classroom*, SpringerBriefs in Psychology 1,
DOI 10.1007/978-3-319-13120-7_7

Life Must Have Meaning

Sixty-nine percent of teachers in the US report that students' lack of interest in learning, or low motivation, is the biggest problem with which they must contend in the classroom (Bridgeland, Bruce, & Hariharan, 2013). Students who lack interest are quickly bored. van Tilburg and Igou (2012) were interested in what it was that makes student boredom different from other emotional experiences. They determined that boredom makes the individual feel that what they do in situations lacking meaning. Boredom is experienced more than sad, angry, or frustrated emotions under these circumstances.

Boredom is related to life satisfaction (Farmer & Sundberg, 1986). This led Fahlman et al. (2009) to conduct that an experimentally controlled demonstration of the relationship between life meaning and boredom. These researchers found that the two concepts; i.e. life meaning and boredom, were correlated but were not the same. They described the relationship between life meaning and boredom as "highly contingent" (p. 335). Fahlman et al. (2009) found that changing individuals perceptions of life meanings could have a positive effect on boredom. Changing perceptions worked well; whereas, trying to manipulate the moods of individuals did not help. School-based mental health workers have the training needed to address student perceptions.

A series of experimental, longitudinal, and quasi-experimental studies have demonstrated that having a purpose for learning is strongly related to self-regulation when students are working on academic tasks (Yeager et al., 2014). Working with low income, predominately racial minority high school students, researchers emphasized that school tasks must be meaningful or students will interpret them as boring. Students who had more purpose in a learning situation persisted for a longer time on a boring task. Instead of telling students to focus on making money, students' personal goals such as contributing to others were fostered. In this study students wrote about social injustices and how the world could be a better place. The goal was to be persuasive without threatening student autonomy, and yet convey a social norm about a self-transcendent purpose for learning. This one-time intervention affected achievement positively by increasing student grades. The intervention additionally doubled the amount of time students spent on test review questions that had no immediate payoff, and increased the number of math problems students solved. Self-regulation was positively affected. Researchers were able to change students' perceptions that specific tasks were meaningless and had no relationship to the their own lives. Students with a stronger purpose for learning persisted longer on the boring tasks. Researchers demonstrated that a brief, one-time psychological intervention, promoting a self-transcendent purpose for learning, could improve high school science and math GPA over several months.

Others have addressed this precursor to boredom (lack of meaning). Hulleman and Harackiewicz (2009) instructed ninth grade students to write about the value and usefulness of the material they were working on in class every few weeks. Making science class personally relevant had the effect of increasing student grades.

Yeager and Bundick (2009) found that diverse 6th, 9th, and 12th grade students with well defined goals felt that they had more meaning in life and in schoolwork in general than their classmates.

Attributional Retraining

Attributions can have a significant effect on academic achievement (Banks & Woolfson, 2008). Negative attributions are associates of low self-esteem. Attributional or explanatory thinking has to do with attributing various factors to success or failure in achievement settings (Perry, Stupnisky, Daniels, & Haynes, 2008). Attributional thinking effects student motivation and working toward goals. In a study of the transition from high school to college, researchers found that students attributed failure to low effort, test difficulty, using ineffective strategies, ineffective teachers, natural ability, and bad luck ... in this order. Clearly, students attributed poor performance to multiple rather than single causes. The group of students least likely to function well were the students who had low expectations of success, took less responsibility for performance, and experienced more negative emotions (anger, shame, guilt, and helplessness). Students, who were most likely to succeed, attributed difficulty to lack of effort. These students evidenced controllable attributions and had a good chance to improve their performance using volitional strategies. The findings of this study may be applicable to other transitions that students experience such as the transition from middle to high school. It is important that students at-risk for, or already exhibiting achievement difficulties, develop mastery attributions which involve effort and strategy use.

Attributional retraining (AR) is a motivation-enhancing treatment designed to offset the dysfunctional explanatory thinking that can arise from unsatisfactory learning experiences (Haynes, Perry, Stupnisky, & Daniels, 2009). Reappraisal and attributional retraining is a promising intervention for boredom. Attributional retraining is designed to improve motivation and emotional variables in student learning and can be applied in the classroom and also to small groups receiving counseling services (Robertson, 2000). Studies of attributional retraining specifically have involved students with learning or emotional disabilities, or both. Students with learning difficulties are more likely to display negative attributions than their classmates without disabilities (Tabassam & Grainger, 2002), although attributional retraining has had a positive effect on the educational performance of high school girls (Lavasani, Sharifian, Naghizadeh, & Hematirad, 2012). Attributional retraining would help students feel more in control (Pekrun et al., 2010). Attributional retraining may be particularly important for low achieving minority students.

Robertson (2000) reviewed 20 studies involving attribution training. These studies involved school-aged children with difficulties in learning. Important variables in training included a focus on the effects of effort, including specific instruction in strategies, and working with small groups as compared to entire classrooms.

Attributional retraining for individuals or small groups may be more successful than full classroom application (Hall & Goetz, 2013, p. 110). This type of intervention fits the role of school psychologists rather than teachers, although Carlyon (1997) suggests that incorporating attributional retraining into social skills training approaches is promising (p. 70) and social skills training can be implemented in the classroom. Also, in class, teachers can help by providing written attributional feedback when correcting student work, to help students attribute successes and failures to insufficient effort and/or lack of use of strategies rather than ability (Robertson, 2000). Attributional retraining may work better for students who are optimistic (Ruthig, Perry, Hall, & Hladkyj, 2004).

More recently, researchers used the combination of attribution retraining with strategy instruction and this combination has resulted in a large effect size that was maintained over 6 weeks (Berkeley, Mastropieri, & Scruggs, 2011). When attributional training is added to strategy instruction, students are more likely to use strategies in the classroom. They also retain the strategies. Generalization improves and attributional beliefs improve (Borkowski, Carr, Rellinger, & Pressley, 2013, p. 76). Intensive strategy training alone is less successful. Attributional beliefs need to be changed to effect student effort. Attributional retraining enhances mastery goals along with reducing helplessness and instilling hopefulness (Daniels et al., 2009). Carr and Borkowski (1989) taught students learning strategies along with attributional training to underachieving children and found that effort increased with strategy-plus-attribution training. Remediation for students in eighth and ninth grade that included a reading comprehension strategy along with attribution retraining has been shown to be successful (Berkeley et al., 2011). The addition of attribution retraining to the academic intervention allowed students to maintain a large effect size in this study. A test of the effects of a brief self-affirming writing assignment was conducted in a sample of middle-school students testing an environmental enhancement to the writing exercise (Bowen, Wegmann, & Webber, 2013). The combination of the affirming writing assignment with an environmental enhancement had *superior effects* to the writing assignment alone.

Bowen et al. (2013) conducted a version of this study. They asked sixth, seventh, and eighth grade students to write a 15-min essay about a value, belief, talent, or skill, about which they were proud. All of the students in this study were from an urban low performing school. They hypothesized that if teachers read the student's essays, this would increase the effects of the intervention particularly if teachers' beliefs and attitudes toward students changed as a result of learning personal information about the students. Students wrote either a self-affirming essay or a neutral essay. Teachers either read the essays or they did not, forming four groups. The middle school decline in grades, in the single core subject involved, did not occur for students in the affirming group. In spite of the fact that no booster sessions were administered as in the Cohen et al. study above, the single administration of the intervention in the fall had benefits that lasted until the end of the school year. Students writing affirming essays that were read by their teacher benefitted most.

Social-Psychological Interventions and Diverse Students

Randomized experiments have found that brief social-psychological interventions targeting students' thoughts, feelings, and beliefs in and about school result in significant increases in student achievement (Yeager & Walton, 2011). These interventions are designed to change beliefs that that they belong, and are valued in school, with the goal of increasing engagement. These brief interventions use persuasive approaches, the goal of which students are unaware, to change thinking and emotions. Yeager and Walton warn that unless these interventions, which appear simplistic on the surface, are implemented correctly, they will not work. Students need to be blind to the purpose of the intervention. If teachers directly told students why schoolwork was important or had value, the interventions would not work in the same way or might have a negative effect. Students must determine personally how content has value for them. Implementing the intervention in a disruptive classroom where students are aware of other students' responses would interfere with the various interventions. Many of the interventions involve writing an essay. The written work must reflect the student's own thoughts. The adult who administers the intervention can make a positive or negative difference in its effect on students. It is advised that should any of the various interventions be implemented that the Yeager and Walton article be carefully reviewed.

Cohen, Garcia, Purdie-Vaughns, and Brzustoski (2009) designed a values-affirmation intervention for three cohorts of African American middle school students. Early in grade seven, students were asked to write about an important personal value or interest in a series of structured writing tasks. At the end each cohort's eighth grade year, students' grade point averages in four core courses were collected. Average GPAs over 2 years were positively affected for the African American but not for the control group of European American students. The effect was greatest for low-performing African American students. The typical drop in grades for middle school students was slowed throughout middle school for these students. The self-perceived adequacy of African American students who did not receive the intervention was lower at the end of the year than at the beginning of the year. The early failure for these students had negative psychological effects.

Attributional retraining was implemented by using college students as mentors for seventh grade low and middle-income Black and Hispanic students. Girls math scores rose as a result on statewide standardized tests, and boys and girls reading scored increased (Good, Aronson, & Inzlicht, 2003). In still another study, seventh graders who were assigned to a values-affirmation condition wrote about social belonging and were compared with those assigned to a control condition. Writing about belonging improved the grade point average (GPA) of Black, but not White students. The more female participants wrote about belonging, the better they performed, while there was no effect of writing about belonging for males (Shnabel, Purdie-Vaughns, Cook, Garcia, & Cohen, 2013).

Stereotyped Threat

A feeling of belonging in school or in a classroom is a critical determinant of academic achievement and persistence, particularly for students of color. This group of students is generally more susceptible to shaky feelings of belonging than White students (Mallett et al., 2011). African American, American Indian, and Latino adolescents experience a decreased sense of school belonging when they are reminded that they belong to a marginalized group. Stereotype threat not only affects school belonging, but also cognitive processing and performance on standardized tests in the case of African American students. When students are aware of stereotypical low expectations, they actually perform less well on tests (Jordan & Lovett, 2007). Stereotype threat effects academic motivations, and intrinsic motivation as well (Thoman, Smith, Brown, Chase, & Lee, 2013). Interventions to target and counter stereotype threat have the possibility of closing the achievement gap (Bowen et al., 2013).

Blackwell et al. (2007) worked with seventh grade primarily minority students in groups of 12–14 students. Students participated in an 8-week workshop in which they learned about the physiology of the brain, study skills, and anti-stereotypic thinking (p. 254). One group of students discussed academic issues of interest to them and half were taught that intelligence is malleable through *incremental theory training*. Incremental theory training teaches that intelligence is malleable. This training resulted in increased motivation in math classes as measured by teacher reports. The group had no decline in math during the semester as compared to the group that did not receive the intervention. Students' theories about their intelligence when they enter junior high in this case was related to their grades during the next 2 years of schooling. It is at the junior high level or most likely the middle school level when schoolwork becomes challenging, that student's theories of intelligence affect academic achievement. As students' beliefs become salient, they are linked to goals, beliefs about effort, attributions, and reactions to challenge. Importantly, these meaning systems that students adopt can be changed.

If these interventions are combined with supportive racial norms, it could make a difference. In ethnically diverse urban middle schools, supportive racial norms affect sense of belonging and academic identity. There is a strong connection between the racial climate of the school and school belonging for Asian, Latino, and White youth (Kogachi, 2013). However, the relationship between racial climate and academic identify was strongest for Latino and African-American students.

Motivational Regulation

Students' apparent lack of motivation is a result of whether or not a student is committed to the teacher's goals in a course, whether or not the student can maintain interest in the course material, the differing value of various components of a course to the student, and the student's ability to *just get through* assignments (McCann & Turner, 2004).

Wolters and Rosenthal (2000) were interested in the relationship between students' motivational beliefs and use of strategies directed toward sustaining or increasing effort and persistence when working on school tasks. Students must initially set goals and then must regulate their engagement in tasks. They need to overcome motivational barriers such as distractions, the increasing difficulty of tasks, tasks that become increasingly boring, or having to work on or engage with material that is irrelevant or unimportant from their point of view. Studies of self-regulated learning do not always distinguish between motivational and volitional processes, which makes the task of locating effective interventions challenging.

Researchers are interested in the strategies that students can use to regulate their effort and persistence when working on school tasks. Garcia and Pintrich (1994) listed a group of motivational regulation strategies. These included self-handicapping strategies such as defensive pessimism and attributional style. Wolters and Rosenthal (2000) looked at five specific strategies. These included; self-consequating strategies, environmental control, interest enhancement, and self-talk (mastery and performance). Wolters and Rosenthal (2000) demonstrated that students with learning goals were more likely to use various motivational strategies, and were less likely to let boredom, distractions, and tasks that become more and more difficult, stop them from completing work. These students used strategies such as reminding themselves about getting good grades, or doing better than classmates. Although this strategy reflects *performance* goals, it was not a deterrent for this group of students. It is important to keep in mind that students need to understand how and when to use strategies before they will be effective. Training in motivational strategies gives students tools they can use to regulate their own effort when completing schoolwork.

Wolters, Pintrich, and Karabenick (2003) evaluated the strategies that could be used to assess students' regulation of their cognition, motivation, and behavior. They also developed scales for assessing the regulation of motivation and behavior. The several groups of strategies they included were mastery self-talk, relevance enhancement, situational interest enhancement, performance/relative ability self-talk, performance/extrinsic self-talk, self-consequating (I tell myself I can do something), and environmental structuring. These are strategies that mental health workers may find useful for specific students.

Motivation is a 'facet' of self-regulation (Fritea & Fritea, 2013, p. 136). Motivational regulation describes a student's effort to increase one's own motivation and to maintain motivation while working on school tasks. Students generate motivational regulation strategies in order to regulate effort, when learning motivational beliefs and attitudes must be turned into effort and persistence so that the student can be successful. There are a number of strategies that students employ in order to regulate motivation and can be taught to students who do not know or use them (see Table 7.1).

The Fritea and Fritea study was the first to investigate boredom in connection with motivational regulation strategies. They found that boredom interferes with

Table 7.1 Strategies for regulating motivation

• Self-consequating is a strategy that a student might use to give him/herself consequences for engaging in learning (personally meaningful incentives or rewards)
• Students may use environmental control strategies to reduce distraction by arranging their surroundings to make a task easier, or to move away from chattering classmates
• A student can regulate his or own motivation by stating a goal, or a reason, for working in class or for finishing a task
• Goal-oriented self-talk is a strategy students might use in which they subvocalize self-encouragement
• Mastery self-talk is related to use of strategies that improve planning, monitoring use of strategies, and effort
• Performance self-talk would be connected to a strategy such as rehearsal. Interest enhancement is a strategy to regulate motivation that works when students try to make the work more interesting or more enjoyable

Source: Fritea and Fritea (2013)

achievement when students aren't using motivational regulation strategies associated with goals. Extrinsic regulation, and activating performance goals such as getting good grades or doing better than one's peers, can increase effort on boring or irrelevant school tasks. Metacognitive skills training to teach motivation regulation strategies would protect students from the effects of negative emotions.

Emotional-Regulation and Volitional Strategy Training

Pekrun and Stephens (2009) suggest that there are a number of approaches to help students regulate emotions in academic situations (see Table 7.2).

Some (or many) students need to be directly taught self-regulated approaches to learning, particularly in adolescence, when students with less self-control than their peers may be vulnerable in situations to which they react emotionally (Casey & Caudle, 2013). Mental health professionals can help students develop self-regulatory skills and this will also improve students' emotional development (Pekrun, 2006).

The emotion-regulation strategies that are typically used in everyday functioning include: reflection, reappraisal, rumination, distraction, expressive suppression, and social sharing (Brans, Koval, Verduyn, Lim, & Kuppens, 2013, p. 927). Socially shared regulation of emotion and learning is new concept. It refers to the ways in which group members regulate their collective activity (Järvelä, Järvenoja, Malmberg, & Hadwin, 2013). Distraction and reflection are the most commonly used emotion regulation strategies, while reappraisal was least used, although reappraisal may be used more than distraction when situations are only mildly negative. Reflection is an adaptive strategy in that it results in positive emotions; whereas, rumination and expressive suppression result in increasing negative emotions. Distraction can be used quickly although once stressed, distraction may require a large investment in concentration and energy. Reflection, reappraisal, and distraction

Table 7.2 Approaches to helping students regulate academic emotions

1.	Emotion-oriented regulation (example: using relaxation techniques)
2.	Reappraisal and attributional retraining
3.	Changing achievement goals and achievement-related beliefs which in turn influence appraisals and emotions
4.	Competency training targeting subject matter knowledge or study strategies
5.	Self-selecting adequate tasks and academic environments that match individual goals and competencies
6.	Making better use of task materials and environments by seeking help
7.	Regulating environments by changing tasks and the achievement climate in classrooms

Source: Pekrun and Stephens (2009, p. 362)

did not decrease negative emotions in the Brans et al. study. Individuals typically use several strategies at a time when they need to control their emotions. Individuals who may be less flexible have difficulty shifting emotions. Individuals who are more flexible cope better with stress. Over-focusing on feelings is not adaptive. Additional common strategies that are used to regulate emotion include: situation selection, in which the individual may decide to avoid a stress inducing setting; situation modification, which may involve thinking about the situation in a different way that is less stressful; distancing; and acceptance.

Turner and Husman (2008) found that the students in their study who were self-regulating used volitional strategies, which researchers felt helped them become engaged and maintain engagements in their classes. Volitional or self-discipline strategies are particularly important when faced with challenge or failure. Volition is an important factor of self-regulation (Corno, 1994). Volitional strategies are related to the use of rehearsal, elaboration, organization, and critical thinking (McCann & Turner, 2004).

Individual differences in volitional regulation have to do with differences in approach-avoidance motivation in achievement situations. Approach-motivated students are more successful (Bartels, Magun-Jackson, & Kemp, 2009). Students with high self-efficacy and who believe that they are capable in a course or subject area, are more interested in the content being delivered, and are more persistent. The student with low self-efficacy and inadequate strategies needs coping strategies to deal with stress. Students who have high fear of failure have to use energy to deal with distracting thoughts or worry and this interferes with using motivational and regulation strategies. Encouraging or teaching the volitional regulation strategies suggested above could be very helpful to students who need them.

It is also important to remember that not all students need volitional strategies very often, and not all strategies would be equally successful for all types of students in the wide variety of learning environments in schools (Dewitte & Lens, 1999), so training in volitional strategies would be best used with small groups of students and must be related to specific subject areas. Mental health workers in schools, such as school psychologists, can help students identify distractions, identify effective and non-effective ways to handle them, teach refocusing which is an effective strategy, and direct students in role-play in which they must handle distracting situations (Corno, 1994). Students must then be monitored by teachers who would be asked to look for evidence that students were actually using strategies, or by measuring time on task.

When a student uses strategies to regulate emotions, motivation, and cognition in order to reach goals, this student is demonstrating volitional control (Bartels et al., 2009). Volitional control focuses attention on goals and helps students maintain effort when trying to reach a goal, particularly when something is interfering with that effort. Motivation, on the other hand, is needed for an individual student to set goals and to choose strategies for reaching goals. The volitional regulation strategies that a student might be taught to maintain effort include:

- positive thinking in regard to self-efficacy or one's capabilities;
- thinking about past successes;
- stress-reducing actions to reduce anxiety; and
- negative incentives, such as how bad one, or significant others, would feel if the effort resulted in disappointment or failure.

Additional broad based strategies to teach provided by Heiss, Ziegler, Engbert, Gropel, and Brand (2010) include:

- reframing the action needed as attractive or positive;
- disengaging from a negative mood if it is interfering;
- focusing attention on what is most relevant;
- choosing goals that are effective;
- increasing speed of decision-making to avoid ruminating; and
- disengaging from thoughts of possible failure.

Corno and Kanfer (1993) divided volitional strategies into overt and covert strategies. Overt strategies involve controlling the tasks of others, and covert strategies include metacognitive strategies, emotion regulation strategies, and motivation strategies. Examples of overt strategies that students can be taught and then encouraged to use may include: making lists of tasks and goals, letting the teacher know when the student is confused, asking peers to stop bothering them when they are working on a task, or asking for help. Examples of covert strategies to be taught and then used might include: using a checklist to go over work before it is handed in; using self talk to stay on task, and to complete tasks, as well as to deal with distractions; using self-instruction; thinking of something that makes one feel better when upset; reminding oneself of past successes; using anxiety reduction strategies; paying attention to one's breathing when stressed; and using imagination to picture oneself being successful. Mental health professionals and teachers can give students the message that involvement can serve as an incentive to use volitional or self discipline strategies (Turner & Husman, 2008). They can encourage students to talk about what works for them and what doesn't work for them (McCann & Turner, 2004). Motivation psychologists examine what a student is thinking and feeling during or after the activity of listening in class, or completing homework, and the thoughts and emotional reactions that are related to the activity (Graham & Weiner, 2013).

Students need to keep records of strategies that work well for them as a journaling activity after major assignments.

An interesting consideration is that self-regulation occurs at the individual student level, and also at the group level, when cooperative learning takes place (Pekrun, 2006). Students work in small groups in the classroom at times. When working in a group, each member of the group shares the responsibility to regulate the atmosphere in which the group is working (Järvenoja, 2010). Each student uses self-regulation strategies, and also must use shared strategies, to overcome social-emotional conflicts. Both forms of regulation play a role in collaborative learning situations. In social learning situations, students must regulate their emotions together, so that they can maintain a goal-oriented process of learning (Järvenoja, 2010). This is a different process than self-regulation or co-regulation in which self-regulation is supported by others. Together, students formulate joint goals and make efforts that get the task accomplished. Students construct motivation together. As students self-regulate, their sense of competence improves and they feel more positive. Positive peer interactions and positive behavioral engagement can facilitate social regulation (Rogat & Linnenbrink-Garcia, 2011). Cooperative learning may allow students to feel more engaged unless the group places a particular student at a disadvantage. Cooperative groups need to be very carefully designed.

Training Attention

Researchers have known that attention is related to boredom for a long time. Wasson in 1981 recommended that an effective strategy to deal with misbehavior at school might be to focus on the internal causes of boredom. Wasson proposed that boredom may be due to inattention. He felt that the effort to sustain the high 'cognitive workload' that a student needs in order to sustain attention could result in fluctuating arousal states. Wasson thought that mindfulness meditation might decrease boredom. *Mindfulness* training teaches students to attend in the present moment (Jha, Krompinger, & Baime, 2007). Mindfulness training has been shown to improve attention and self-regulation (Tang & Posner, 2009). MacLean et al. (2010) demonstrated that extensive training using meditation, in which participants concentrated on their breathing, could improve sustained attention. The integrative body-mind training method, combines meditation and mindfulness (Tang et al., 2007). Five days of training using this approach was demonstrated to be helpful in lowering negative emotions and improving attention and self-regulation. Researchers found that an 8-week mindfulness-based stress reduction (MBSR) course improved orientation skills. Although longer and more intensive training had better results, an 8-week intervention could reasonably be implemented in schools.

LePera (2011) studied the relationship between boredom proneness and mindfulness. LePera hypothesized that mindfulness may be a mediator between attention and negative outcomes. If this is the case, mindfulness training might provide interventions for boredom proneness given mindfulness training has been demonstrated to be helpful in ameliorating anxiety, and in increasing emotional wellbeing. Mindfulness appears to improve both internal and external attention and possibly could improve the tendency to decrease internal distractions. LePera also noted that the inability of some individuals to label their moods may need to be improved as well. This supports the need for training in emotion vocabulary.

Exercises using a computer have been found to be helpful for children and adults improving attention (Tang & Posner, 2009). Interventions for groups of students to improve attention skills are under study, but other than mindfulness training, may not yet be ready for implementation in K-12 schools.

Boredom Coping

High school students engage in more avoidance coping than college students (Zeidner, 1996), and so it is particularly important to encourage effective coping strategies in K-12 students. Students need to be taught what to do when they feel anxious and what to do when they feel bored (Furner & Gonzalez-DeHass, 2011). There are many anxiety reduction strategies that mental health professionals know well that can be taught to students. Boredom coping strategies may be less well known. Traditional ways to cope with boredom have involved giving students choices, or increasing the stimulation of lecture or reading material (Martin, Sadlo, & Stew, 2006). Increasing physical movement may be helpful as well, but these are not things students themselves can control in a classroom situation. Instead, students may disengage when bored, and talk to a classmate who is nearby, or ask to leave the class to go to the bathroom, or play with their mobile phone, or doodle, or read a book hidden under their desktops, or daydream.

Researchers recommend that it would be more effective to focus on internal causes of boredom rather than external causes (Martin et al., 2006). This approach might address students' difficulties sustaining attention, or for those students having more extensive difficulties dealing with boredom, mental health professionals in schools could teach coping strategies. Some students will need direct training in coping with the emotion of boredom (Pekrun et al., 2010).

Todman (2003) suggested that covert boredom coping skills should be integrated into the social skills training, particularly for individuals experiencing distractibility and/or mood disorders. Coping skills can be taught in small groups although there are few curricula that include coping with boredom. For example, the *SkillStreaming* series (McGinnis & Goldstein, 1997) includes a single lesson on dealing with boredom and only at the elementary level. The skill includes: using time wisely, time management, and organization; and, suggesting productive alternatives to having nothing to do. However, it does not specifically address boredom in school. The PATHS curriculum, Promoting Alternative Thinking Strategies (Greenberg, Kusche, Cook, & Quamma, 1995), teaches students how to handle emotions positively and this is one of only a few curricula shown to improve executive functioning at least in young children (Diamond, 2012).

In searching for ways to directly teach boredom coping skills, it is necessary to first understand what students already do to cope with boredom. A study of students in grades 5–10 identified four categories of coping strategies (Nett et al., 2011). These included two approach strategies, and two avoidance strategies. The approach and avoidance coping strategies can be considered both cognitive and behavioral. Students who utilized a *cognitive approach strategy* focused on what might be valuable in the material being presented, such as how it might help them reach career goals. For example, students might tell themselves that the content is important, and might increase their efforts to pay attention (Daniels & Tze, 2014). The cognitive approach strategy requires the students to change their perceptions of the classroom situation. Use of cognitive approach strategies in studies has resulted in the largest decrease in boredom. Students who use *behavioral approach strategies* tend to try to change the situation by asking the teacher for different tasks, or by asking the teacher to change activities. This strategy, if misinterpreted by the teacher, or if the teacher isn't open to change, can disrupt class activity and negatively effect classmates' concentration. Students who used *cognitive avoidance strategies* in studies have used distraction. Students engaged in thinking about something that *did* interest them, instead of thinking about the content of what the teacher was presenting. Students who used *behavioral avoidance* also used distraction, but did so by engaging in actions such as talking with classmates, flirting with peers, passing notes, or skipping class altogether. Students who are aware of the fact that others may not perceive the same classroom content or subject boring, or as boring as they do, may be in a better position to change their perceptions. Students who believe that the class is boring because the lesson or the teaching is boring, tend to use avoidance strategies.

Nett et al. (2011) developed a research tool to measure the four strategies to cope with boredom in the classroom, in the form of a questionnaire. For each of the four categories, five items serve as representative samples of the strategies. The resulting 20 items formed a scale that was piloted with students. Because boredom is content specific, the questionnaire refers to boredom coping strategies associated with mathematics.

Also because students typically used more than one strategy, Nett and colleagues took the data they had collected and grouped students demonstrating different patterns of use of strategies. They found three different groups. The students they called the '*Reappraisers*' used cognitive approach strategies most often, and experienced less boredom than the students who used avoidance strategies. The students labeled '*Criticizers*' used behavioral approach strategies most often. They let the teacher know that they were frustrated. The third group the '*Evaders*' would rather avoid the feelings of boredom than try to change anything. Avoidance coping is related to depressive symptoms.

Learning-related boredom affects all students and is valid across school settings in several different cultures (Tze, Klassen, Daniels, Li, & Zhang, 2013). However Tze (2011) found, using the Nett et al. data, boredom had different effects when studying depending on culture, and western versus non-western academic settings. Canadian college-age students tended to cope with boredom in school by using cognitive-approach coping. Chinese students preferred avoidance coping.

Daniels and Tze (2014) were interested in which coping strategies teachers would want their students to use. The coping strategies they considered included: a *cognitive approach* which involved self-talk; *cognitive avoidance*, which involved distraction by thinking of something unrelated to the class; *behavioral approach*, which could involve asking the teacher to do something else; or *behavioral avoidance*, such as passing notes, reading unrelated material, or pretending to be sick and leaving class. They surveyed both elementary and secondary Canadian teachers. The teachers ranked cognitive-approach strategies highest as teachers realized that this strategy was most effective, and would also result in little disruption to teaching or learning. Importantly, teachers ranked behavioral-approach strategies next, in spite of the fact that this might result in additional work for the teacher, who would need to make adaptations in teaching approach by actively trying to change the boring material or teaching approach. Students would not use behavioral approach strategies if they thought that the teacher would not respond positively, or if in the past the teacher had not responded positively. Teachers who understand boredom can be partners in helping school psychologists, and other mental health school-based professionals, address student disengagement and inattention.

School psychologists can work with individual students or small groups of students to teach specific boredom coping skills such as goal-oriented self-talk (Fritea & Fritea, 2013). Goal-oriented self-talk is a skill in which students talk to themselves while they are working on a 'boring' activity. Mastery self-talk has been demonstrated to be associated with valuing academic tasks. In addition, it has been related to use of cognitive strategies for learning. Goal-oriented self-talk is a motivational regulation strategy.

In the past, boredom in the classroom was neglected. When it was addressed, teachers were targeted as not presenting interesting material, or not using engaging teaching techniques. Researchers now view the experience of boredom as both internally and externally generated. Researchers today take boredom seriously albeit more so in countries other than the US at this point in time. Much of the research is directed toward decreasing the experience of boredom in college-aged students and this needs to change. Although Nett et al. (2011) tell us that boring situations cannot be avoided for every student, in every class, or all the time, given the prevalence of student boredom in school-age populations, and the very serious consequences when boredom is neglected, it is time for open discussions around boredom to take place in public schools, and for school psychologists and other mental health workers to get involved in those discussions.

References

Abramson, L. Y., Metalsky, G. I., & Alloy, L. B. (1989). Hopelessness depression: A theory-based subtype of depression. *Psychological Review, 96*(2), 358–372. doi:10.1037/0033-295X.96.2.358.

Acee, T. W., Kim, H., Kim, H. J., Kim, J., Chu, H. R., Kim, M., ... Riekenberg, J. J. (2010). Academic boredom in under- and over-challenging situations. *Contemporary Educational Psychology, 35*(1), 17–27. doi:10.1016/j.cedpsych.2009.08.002.

Ahmed, W., van der Werf, G., Kuyper, H., & Minnaert, A. (2013). Emotions, self-regulated learning, and achievement in mathematics: A growth curve analysis. *Journal of Educational Psychology, 105*(1), 150–161. doi:10.1037/a0030160.

Ainley, M. (2006). Connecting with learning: Motivation, affect and cognition in interest processes. *Educational Psychology Review, 18*, 391–405. doi:10.1007/s10648-006-9033-0.

Ainley, M. (2010). Interest in the dynamics of task behavior: Processes that link person and task in effective learning. In T. Urdan & S. A. Karabenick (Eds.), *Advances in motivation and achievement: The next decade of research in motivation and achievement* (Vol. 16A, pp. 235–264). Bingley, England: Emerald Group.

Ainley, M. (2012). Students' interest and engagement in classroom activities. In S. L. Christenson, A. L. Reschly, & C. Wylie (Eds.), *Handbook of research on student engagement* (pp. 283–302). New York, NY: Springer.

Amsterlaw, J., Lagattuta, K. H., & Meltzoff, A. N. (2009). Young children's reasoning about the effects of emotional and physiological states on academic performance. *Child Development, 80*(1), 115–133. doi:10.1111/j.1467-8624.2008.01249.x.

Appleton, J. J., Christenson, S. L., Kim, D., & Reschly, A. L. (2006). Measuring cognitive and psychological engagement: Validation of the Student Engagement Instrument. *Journal of School Psychology, 44*(5), 427–445. doi:10.1016/j.jsp.2006.04.002.

Arsenio, W. F., & Loria, S. (2014). Coping with negative emotions: Connections with adolescents' academic performance and stress. *Journal of Genetic Psychology, 175*(1), 76–90. doi:10.1080/00221325.2013.806293.

Ashcraft, M. J. (2002). Math anxiety: Personal, educational, and cognitive consequences. *Current Directions in Psychological Science, 11*(5), 181–185. doi:10.1111/1467-8721.00196.

Assor, A., Kaplan, H., Kanat-Maymon, Y., & Roth, G. (2005). Directly controlling teacher behaviors as predictors of poor motivation and engagement in girls and boys: The role of anger and anxiety. *Learning and Instruction, 15*(5), 397–413. doi:10.1016/j.learninstruc.2005.07.008.

Baker, R. S., D'Mello, S. K., Rodrigo, M. T., & Graesser, A. C. (2010). Better to be frustrated than bored: The incidence, persistence, and impact of learners' cognitive-affective states during interactions with three different computer-based learning environments. *International Journal of Human-Computer Studies, 68*(4), 223–241. doi:10.1016/j.ijhcs.2009.12.003.

© Springer International Publishing Switzerland 2015
G.L. Macklem, *Boredom in the Classroom*, SpringerBriefs in Psychology 1,
DOI 10.1007/978-3-319-13120-7

Banks, M., & Woolfson, L. (2008). Why do students think they fail? The relationship between attributions and academic self-perceptions. *British Journal of Special Education, 35*(1), 49–56. doi:10.1111/j.1467-8578.2008.00369.x.

Barnett, L. A., & Klitzing, S. W. (2006). Boredom in free time: Relationships with personality, affect, and motivation for different gender, racial, and ethnic student groups. *Leisure Science, 28*, 223–244. doi:10.1080/01490400600598053.

Bartels, J. M., Magun-Jackson, S., & Kemp, A. D. (2009). Volitional regulation and self-regulated learning: An examination of individual differences in approach-avoidance achievement motivation. *Electronic Journal of Research in Educational Psychology, 7*(18), 605–626. Retrieved from http://www.redalyc.org

Baumeister, R. F., Bratslavsky, E., Muraven, M., & Tice, D. M. (1998). Ego depletion: Is the active self a limited resource? *Journal of Personality and Social Psychology, 74*, 1252–1265. doi:10.1037/0022-3514.74.5.1252.

Baumeister, R. F., & Vohs, K. D. (2007). Self-regulation, ego depletion, and motivation. *Social and Personality Psychology Compass, 1*(1), 115–128. doi:10.1111/j.1751-9004.2007.00001.x.

Baumeister, R. F., Vohs, K. D., & Tice, D. M. (2007). The strength model of self-control. *Current Directions in Psychological Science, 16*(6), 351–355. doi:10.1111/j.1467-8721.2007.00534.x.

Beck, L., Kumschick, I. R., Eid, M., & Klann-Delius, G. (2012). Relationship between language competence and emotional competence in middle childhood. *Emotion, 12*(3), 503–514. doi:10.1037/a0026320.

Behnardo, B. I. (2013). Positive academic emotions moderate the relationship between self-regulation and academic achievement. *British Journal of Educational Psychology, 83*(2), 329–340. doi:10.1111/j.2044-8279.2012.02064.x.

Belton, T., & Priyadharshini, E. (2007). Boredom and schooling: A cross-disciplinary exploration. *Cambridge Journal of Education, 37*(4), 579–595. doi:10.1080/03057640701706227.

Bench, S. W., & Lench, H. C. (2013). On the function of boredom. *Behavioral Science, 3*(3), 459–472. doi:10.3390/bs3030459.

Berg, C. (2007). *Academic emotions in student achievement: Promoting engagement and critical thinking through lessons in bioethical dilemmas.* Retrieved from http://www.mcli.dist.maricopa.edu

Berkeley, S., Mastropieri, M. A., & Scruggs, T. E. (2011). Reading comprehension strategy instruction and attribution retraining for secondary students with learning and other mild disabilities. *Journal of Learning Disabilities, 44*(1), 18–32. doi:10.1177/0022219410371677.

Berryhill, J., Linney, J. A., & Fromewick, J. (2009). The effects of education accountability on teachers: Are policies too-stress provoking for their own good? *International Journal of Education Policy and Leadership, 4*(5), 1–14. Retrieved from http://journals.sfu.ca

Bieg, M., Goetz, T., & Lipnevich, A. A. (2014). What students think they feel differs from what they really feel—Academic self-concept moderates the discrepancy between students' trait and state emotional self-reports. *PLoS One, 9*(3), e92563. doi:10.1371/journal.pone.0092563.

Bingham, G. E., & Okagaki, L. (2012). Ethnicity and student engagement. In S. L. Christenson, A. L. Reschly, & C. Wylie (Eds.), *Handbook of research on student engagement* (pp. 65–95). New York, NY: Springer.

Blackwell, L. S., Trzesniewski, K. H., & Dweck, C. S. (2007). Implicit theories of intelligence predict achievement across an adolescent transition: A longitudinal study and an intervention. *Child Development, 78*(1), 246–263. doi:10.1111/j.1467-8624.2007.00995.x.

Blaszczynski, A., McConaghy, N., & Frankova, A. (1990). Boredom proneness in pathological gambling. *Psychological Reports, 67*, 35–42. doi:10.2466/pr0.1990.67.1.35.

Blunt, A., & Pychyl, T. A. (1998). Volitional action and inaction in the lives of undergraduate students: State orientation, procrastination and proneness to boredom. *Personality and Individual Differences, 24*(6), 837–846. doi:10.1016/S0191-8869(98)00018-X.

Bonwell, C. C., & Eison, J. A. (1991). *Active learning: Creating excitement in the classroom* (ASHE–ERIC Higher Education Report No. 1). Washington, DC: The George Washington University, School of Education and Human Development.

Borkowski, J. G., Carr, M., Rellinger, E., & Pressley, M. (2013). Self-regulated cognition: Interdependence of metacognition, attributions, and self-esteem. In B. F. Jones (Ed.), *Dimensions of thinking and cognitive instruction* (pp. 53–92). New York, NY: Routledge.

Boucher, H. C., & Kofos, M. N. (2012). The idea of money counteracts ego depletion effects. *Journal of Experimental Social Psychology, 48*(4), 804–810. doi:10.1016/j.jesp.2012.02.003.

Bowen, N. K., Wegmann, K. M., & Webber, K. C. (2013). Enhancing a brief writing intervention to combat stereotype threat among middle-school students. *Journal of Educational Psychology, 105*(2), 427–435. doi:10.1037/a0031177.

Bowers, A. J., & Sprott, R. (2012). Examining the multiple trajectories associated with dropping out of high school: A growth mixture model analysis. *The Journal of Educational Research, 105*(3), 176–195. doi:10.1080/00220671.2011.552075.

Brackett, M. A., Rivers, S. E., Reyes, M. R., & Salovey, P. (2012). Enhancing academic performance and social and emotional competence with the RULER Feeling Words Curriculum. *Learning and Individual Differences, 22*(2), 218–224. doi:10.1016/j.lindif.2010.10.002.

Brans, K., Koval, P., Verduyn, P., Lim, Y. L., & Kuppens, P. (2013). The regulation of negative and positive affect in daily life. *Emotion, 13*(5), 926–939. doi:10.1037/a0032400.

Bridgeland, J. M., Balfanz, R., Moore, L. A., & Friant, R. S. (2010, March). *Engaging students, teachers, and parents to help end the high school dropout epidemic*. Washington, DC: Civic Enterprises, LLC.

Bridgeland, J., Bruce, M., & Hariharan, A. (2013). *The missing piece: A national teacher survey on how social and emotional learning can empower children and transform schools*. Chicago, IL: Civic Enterprises, with Peter D. Hart Research Associates, for the Collaborative for Academic, Social, and Emotional Learning (CASEL).

Bridgeland, J. M., Dilulio, J. J., & Balfanz, R. (2009, June). *On the front lines of schools: Perspectives of teachers and principals on the high school dropout problems*. Washington, DC: Civic Enterprises, LLC.

Bridgeland, J. M., Dilulio, J. J., & Morison, K. B. (2006). *The silent epidemic: Perspectives of high school dropouts*. Washington, DC: Civic Enterprises, LLC.

Caldwell, L. L., Darling, N., Payne, L. L., & Dowdy, B. (1999). "Why are you bored?": An examination of psychological and social control causes of boredom among adolescents. *Journal of Leisure Research, 31*(2), 103–121. Retrieved from http://js.sagamorepub.com

Carlyon, W. D. (1997). Attribution retraining: Implications for its integration into prescriptive social skills training. *School Psychology Review, 26*(1), 61–73. Retrieved from http://www.nasponline.org

Carr, M., & Borkowski, J. G. (1989). Attributional training and the generalization of reading strategies with underachieving children. *Learning and Individual Differences, 1*(3), 327–341. doi:10.1016/1041-6080(89)90015-0.

Carriere, J. S., Cheyne, J. A., & Smilek, S. (2008). Everyday attention lapses and memory failures: The affective consequences of mindlessness. *Consciousness and Cognition, 17*, 835–847. doi:10.1016/j.concog.2007.04.008.

Casey, B. J., & Caudle, K. (2013). The teenage brain: Self control. *Current Directions in Psychological Science, 22*(2), 82–87. doi:10.1177/0963721413480170.

Cheyne, J. A., Carriere, J. S., & Smilek, D. (2006). Absent-mindedness: Lapses of conscious awareness and everyday cognitive failures. *Consciousness and Cognition, 15*(3), 578–592. doi:10.1016/j.concog.2005.11.009.

Christenson, S. L., Reschly, A. L., & Wylie, C. (2012). Preface. In S. L. Christenson, A. L. Reschly, & C. Wylie, (Eds.), *Handbook of research on students engagement* (pp. v–ix). New York, NY: Springer.

Clarke, M., Shore, A., Rhoades, K., Abrams, L., Miao, J., & Li, J. (2003). *Perceived effects of state-mandated testing programs on teaching and learning: Findings from interviews with educators in low-, medium-, and high-stakes states*. Boston, MA: Lynch School of Education, National Board of Educational Testing and Public Policy. Retrieved from http://www.bc.edu

Cohen, G. L., Garcia, J., Purdie-Vaughns, V., & Brzustoski, P. (2009). Recursive processes in self-affirmation: Intervening to close the minority achievement gap. *Science, 324*, 400–403. doi:10.1126/science.1170769.

Corno, L. (1994). Student volition and education: Outcomes, influences, and practices. In B. J. Zimmerman & D. H. Schunk (Eds.), *Self-regulation of learning and performance* (pp. 229–254). Hillsdale, NJ: Lawrence Erlbaum Associates.

Corno, L., & Kanfer, R. (1993). The role of volition in learning and performance. *Review of Research in Education, 19*, 301–341. Retrieved from http://www.jstor.org

Dahlen, E. R., Martin, R. C., Ragan, K., & Kuhlman, M. M. (2004). Boredom proneness in anger and aggression: Effects of impulsiveness and sensation seeking. *Personality and Individual Differences, 37*(8), 1615–1627. doi:10.1016/j.paid.2004.02.016.

Dahlen, E. R., Martin, R. C., Ragan, K., & Kuhlman, M. M. (2005). Driving anger, sensation seeking, impulsiveness, and boredom proneness in the prediction of unsafe driving. *Accident Analysis & Prevention, 37*(2), 341–348. doi:10.1016/j.aap.2004.10.006.

Damrad-Frye, R., & Laird, J. D. (1989). The experience of boredom: The role of the self-perception of attention. *Journal of Personality & Social Psychology, 57*(2), 315–320. doi:10.1037/0022-3514.57.2.315.

Danckert, J. A., & Allman, A. A. (2005). Time flies when you're having fun: Temporal estimation and the experience of boredom. *Brain and Cognition, 59*(3), 236–245. doi:10.1016/j.bandc.2005.07.002.

Daniels, L. M., Stupnisky, R. H., Pekrun, R., Haynes, T. L., Perry, R. P., & Newall, N. E. (2009). A longitudinal analysis of achievement goals: From affective antecedents to emotional effects and achievement outcomes. *Journal of Educational Psychology, 101*(4), 948–963. doi:10.1037/a0016096.

Daniels, L. M., & Tze, V. M. C. (2014). How do teachers want students to cope with boredom? *ASCDExpress, 9*(8). Retrieved from http://www.ascd.org/ascd-express/vol9/908-daniels.aspx

Daschmann, E. C. (2013). *Boredom in school from the perspectives of students, teachers and parents* (Doctoral dissertation, University of Konstanz, Konstanz, Germany). Retrieved from http://kops.ub.uni-konstanz.de

Daschmann, E. C., Goetz, T., & Stupnisky, R. H. (2011). Testing the predictors of boredom at school: Development and validation of the precursors to boredom scales. *British Journal of Educational Psychology, 81*(Pt. 3), 421–440. doi:10.1348/000709910X526038.

Daschmann, E. C., Goetz, T., & Stupnisky, R. H. (2014). Exploring the antecedents of boredom: Do teachers know why students are bored? *Teaching and Teacher Education, 39*, 22–30. doi:10.1016/j.tate.2013.11.009.

Davies, J., & Fortney, M. (2012). *The Menton theory of engagement and boredom* (pp. 131–143). Poster presented at the First Annual Conference on Advances in Cognitive Systems, Palo Alto, CA. Retrieved from http://www.cogsys.org

Dettmers, S., Trautwein, U., Lüdtke, O., Goetz, T., Frenzel, A. C., & Pekrun, R. (2011). Students' emotions during homework in mathematics: Testing a theoretical model of antecedents and achievement outcomes. *Contemporary Educational Psychology, 36*(1), 25–35. doi:10.1016/j.cedpsych.2010.10.001.

Dettmers, S., Trautwein, U., Lüdtke, O., Kunter, M., & Baumert, J. (2010). Homework works if homework quality is high: Using multilevel modeling to predict the development of achievement in mathematics. *Journal of Educational Psychology, 102*(2), 467–482. doi:10.1037/a0018453.

Dewitte, S., & Lens, W. (1999). Volition: Use with measure. *Learning and Individual Differences, 11*(3), 321–333. doi:10.1016/S1041-6080(99)80006-5.

Diamond, A. (2005). Attention-deficit disorder (attention-deficit/hyperactivity disorder without hyperactivity): A neurobiologically and behaviorally distinct disorder from attention-deficit/hyperactivity disorder (with hyperactivity). *Developmental Psychopathology, 17*(3), 807–825. doi:10.1017/S0954579405050388.

Diamond, A. (2012). Activities and programs that improve children's executive functions. *Current Directions in Psychological Science, 21*(5), 335–341. doi:10.1177/0963721412453722.

Droit-Volet, S., & Meck, W. H. (2007). How emotions colour our perceptions of time. *TRENDS in Cognitive Science, 11*(12), 504–513. doi:10.1016/j.tics.2007.09.008.

Dweck, J. V., & Walton, G. M. (2010). Ego depletion—Is it all in your head? Implicit theories about will power affect self-regulation. *Psychological Science, 21*(11), 1686–1693. doi:10.1177/0956797610384745.

Eastwood, J. D., Cavaliere, C., Fahlman, S. A., & Eastwood, A. E. (2007). A desire for desires: Boredom and its relation to alexithymia. *Personality and Individual Differences, 42*(6), 1035–1045. doi:10.1016/j.paid.2006.08.027.

Eastwood, J. D., Frischen, A., Fenske, M. J., & Smilek, D. (2012). The unengaged mind: Defining boredom in terms of attention. *Perspectives on Psychological Science, 7*(5), 482–495. doi:10.1177/1745691612456044.

Efklides, A., & Volet, S. (2005). Emotional experiences during learning: Multiple, situated, and dynamic. *Learning and Instruction, 15*, 377–380. doi:10.1016/j.learninstruc.2005.07.006.

Fahlman, S. A. (2009). *Development and validation of the Multidimensional State Boredom Scale* (Doctoral dissertation, York University, Ottawa, Canada). Available from ProQuest Dissertations and Thesis. Retrieved from http://www.todmanpsychology.org/

Fahlman, S. A., Mercer, K. B., Gaskovski, P., Eastwood, A. E., & Eastwood, J. D. (2009). Does a lack of life meaning cause boredom? Results from psychometric, longitudinal, and experimental analyses. *Journal of Social and Clinical Psychology, 28*(3), 307–340. doi:10.1521/jscp.2009.28.3.307.

Fahlman, S. A., Mercer-Lynn, K. B., Flora, D. B., & Eastwood, J. D. (2013). Development and validation of the Multidimensional State Boredom Scale. *Assessment, 20*(1), 68–85. doi:10.1177/1073191111421303.

Farb, N. A. S., Chapman, H. A., & Anderson, A. K. (2013). Emotion: Form follows function. *Current Opinion in Neurobiology, 23*(3), 393–398. doi:10.1016/j.conb.2013.01.015.

Farmer, R., & Sundberg, N. D. (1986). Boredom proneness—The development and correlates of a new scale. *Journal of Personality Assessment, 50*(1), 4–17. doi:10.1207/s15327752jpa5001_2.

Farrell, J. B. (2009). Active learning: Theories and research. *Jewish Educational Leadership, 7*(3). Retrieved from http://www.lookstein.org

Faust, M. W., Ashcraft, M. H., & Fleck, D. E. (1996). Mathematics anxiety effects in simple and complex addition. *Mathematical Cognition, 2*, 25–62. doi:10.1080/135467996387534.

Fawcett, L. M. (2007). *School's out: Adolescent' leisure time activities, influences and consequences* (Doctoral dissertation, Edith Cowan University, Perth, Australia). Retrieved from http://ro.ecu.edu.au/theses/31

Feng, L., Figlio, D. N., & Sass, T. R. (2010). School accountability and teacher mobility (NBER Working Paper No. w16070). *Social Science Research Network*. Retrieved from http://papers.ssrn.com

Finn, J. D., & Zimmer, K. S. (2012). Student engagement: What is it? Why does it matter? In S. L. Christenson, A. L. Reschly, & C. Wylie (Eds.), *Handbook of research on student engagement* (pp. 97–131). New York, NY: Springer.

Fisher, C. D. (1998). Effects of external and internal interruptions on boredom at work. Two studies. *Journal of Organizational Behavior, 19*(5), 503–522. doi:10.1002/(SICI)1099-1379.

Fisherl, C. D. (1993). Boredom at work: A neglected concept. *Human Relations, 46*(3), 395–417. doi:10.1177/001872679304600305.

Forgas, J. P. (2013). Don't worry, be sad! On the cognitive, motivations, and interpersonal benefits of negative mood. *Current Directions in Psychological Science, 22*(3), 225–232. doi:10.1177/0963721412474458.

Fredrickson, B. L. (2001). The role of positive emotions in positive psychology: The broaden-and-build theory of positive emotions. *American Psychologist, 56*(3), 218–226. doi:10.1037/0003-066X.56.3.218.

Frenzel, A. C., Pekrun, R., & Goetz, T. (2007). Perceived learning environment and students' emotional experiences: A multilevel analysis of mathematics classrooms. *Learning and Instruction, 17*, 478–493. doi:10.1016/j.learninstruc.2007.09.001.

Fritea, I., & Fritea, R. (2013). Can motivational regulation counteract the effects of boredom on academic achievement? *Procedia—Social and Behavioral Sciences, 78*, 135–139. doi:10.1016/j.sbspro.2013.04.266.

Furner, J. M., & Gonzalez-DeHass, A. (2011). How do students' mastery and performance goals relate to math anxiety? *Eurasia Journal of Mathematics, Science and Technology Education, 7*(4), 227–242. Retrieved from http://www.ejmste.com

Gailliot, M. T., Plant, E. A., Butz, D. A., & Baumeister, R. F. (2007). Increasing self-regulatory strength can reduce the depleting effect of suppressing stereotypes. *Personality and Social Psychology Bulletin, 33*(2), 281–294. doi:10.1177/0146167206296101.

Gana, K., Deletang, B., & Metais, L. (2000). Is boredom proneness associated with introspectiveness? *Social Behavior and Personality: An International Journal, 28*, 499–504. doi:10.2224/sbp.2000.28.5.499.

Garcia, T., & Pintrich, P. R. (1994). Regulating motivation and cognition in the classroom: The role of self-schemas and self-regulatory strategies. In D. H. Schunk & B. J. Zimmerman (Eds.), *Self-regulation of learning and performance: Issues and educational applications* (pp. 127–153). Hillsdale, NJ: Lawrence Erlbaum Associates.

Gendron, M., Lindquist, K. A., Barsalou, L., & Barrett, L. F. (2012). Emotion words shape emotion precepts. *Emotion, 12*(2), 314–325. doi:10.1037/a0026007.

Gibson, G. S., & Morales, F. (1995). *Ethnic and gender differences in boredom proneness* (Tech. Rep.). Oak Ridge, TN: Technical Information Center. Retrieved from http://www.osti.gov/scitech/servlets/purl/184264

Goetz, T., Cronjaeger, H., Frenzel, A. C., Lüdtke, O., & Hall, N. C. (2010). Academic self-concept and emotion relations: Domain specificity and age effects. *Contemporary Educational Psychology, 35*(1), 44–58. doi:10.1016/j.cedpsych.2009.10.001.

Goetz, T., & Frenzel, A. C. (2006). Phenomenology of boredom at school. *Zeitschrift für Entwicklungspsychologie und Pädagogische Psychologie, 38*(4), 149–153. doi:10.1026/0049-8637.38.4.149.

Goetz, T., Frenzel, A. C., Hall, N. C., Nett, U. E., Pekrun, R., & Lipnevich, A. A. (2014). Types of boredom: An experience sampling approach. *Motivation and Emotion, 38*(3), 401–419. doi:10.1007/s11031-013-9385-y.

Goetz, T., Frenzel, A. C., Pekrun, R., Hall, N. C., & Lüdtke, O. (2007). Between- and within-domain relations of students' academic emotions. *Journal of Educational Psychology, 99*(4), 715–733. doi:10.1037/0022-0663.99.4.715.

Goetz, T., Nett, U. E., Martiny, S. E., Hall, N. C., Pekrun, R., Dettmers, S., & Trautwein, U. (2012). Students' emotions during homework: Structures, self-concept antecedents, and achievement outcomes. *Learning and Individual Differences, 22*(2), 225–234. doi:10.1016/j.lindif.2011.04.006

Goetz, T., Pekrun, R., Hall, N., & Haag, L. (2006). Academic emotions from a social-cognitive perspective: Antecedents and domain specificity of students' affect in the context of Latin instruction. *British Journal of Educational Psychology, 76*, 289–308. doi:10.1348/000709905X42860.

Goetz, T., Preckel, F., Pekrun, R., & Hall, N. C. (2007). Emotional experiences during test taking: Does cognitive ability make a difference? *Learning and Individual Differences, 17*(1), 3–16. doi:10.1016/j.lindif.2006.12.002.

Goldberg, Y., & Danckert, J. (2013). Traumatic brain injury, boredom and depression. *Behavioral Sciences, 3*(3), 434–444. doi:10.3390/bs3030434.

Goldberg, Y. K., Eastwood, J. D., LaGuardia, J., & Danckert, J. (2011). Boredom: An emotional experience distinct from apathy, anhedonia, or depression. *Journal of Social and Clinical Psychology, 30*(6), 647–666. doi:10.1521/jscp.2011.30.6.647.

Good, C., Aronson, J., & Inzlicht, M. (2003). Improving adolescents' standardized test performance: An intervention to reduce the effects of stereotype threat. *Applied Developmental Psychology, 24*, 645–662. doi:10.1016/j.appdev.2003.09.002.

Gordon, A., Wilkinson, R., McGown, A., & Jovanoska, S. (1997). The psychometric properties of the boredom proneness scale: An examination of its validity. *Psychological Studies, 42*, 85–97. doi:10.2466/PMS.71.7.963-966.

Graham, S., & Weiner, B. (2013). Motivation: Past, present, and future. In K. R. Harris, S. Graham, T. Urdan, C. B. McCormick, G. M. Sinatra, & J. Sweller (Eds.), *APA educational psychology handbook: Theories, constructs, and critical issues* (Vol. 1, pp. 367–397). Washington, DC: American Psychological Association. doi:10.1037/13273-013.

Greenberg, M. T., Kusche, C. A., Cook, E. T., & Quamma, J. P. (1995). Promoting emotional competence in school-aged children: The effects of the PATHS curriculum. *Development and Psychopathology, 7*(1), 117–136. doi:10.1017/S0954579400006374.

Gregory, A., Allen, J. P., Mikami, A. Y., Hafen, C. A., & Pianta, R. C. (2014). Effects of a professional development program on behavioral engagement of students in middle and high school. *Psychology in the Schools, 51*(2), 143–163. doi:10.1002/pits.21741.

Grund, A., Brassier, N. K., & Fries, S. (2014). Torn between study and leisure: How motivational conflicts related to students' academic and social adaptation. *Journal of Educational Psychology, 106*(1), 242–257. doi:10.1037/a0034400.

Gumora, G., & Arsenio, W. F. (2002). Emotionality, emotion regulation, and school performance in middle school children. *Journal of School Psychology, 40*, 395–413. doi:10.1016/S0022-4405(02) 00108-5.

Guthrie, J. T., Coddington, C. S., & Wigfield, A. (2009). Profiles of reading motivation among African American and Caucasian students. *Journal of Literacy Research, 41*, 317–353. doi:10.1080/10862960903129196.

Hagger, M. S., Wood, C., Stiff, C., & Chatzisarantis, N. L. D. (2010). Ego depletion and the strength model of self-control: A meta-analysis. *Psychological Bulletin, 136*(4), 495–525. doi:10.1037/a0019486.

Hall, N. C., & Goetz, T. (2013). *Emotion, motivation, and self-regulation: A handbook for teachers* (pp. 57–122). Bingley, England: Emerald Group Publishing Limited.

Harris, M. B. (2000). Correlates and characteristics of boredom proneness and boredom. *Journal of Applied Social Psychology, 30*, 576–598. doi:10.1111/j.1559-1816.2000.tb02497.x.

Haynes, T. L., Perry, R. P., Stupnisky, R. H., & Daniels, L. M. (2009). A review of attributional retraining treatments: Fostering engagement and persistence in vulnerable college students. In M. B. Paulsen (Ed.), *Higher education: Handbook of theory and research* (pp. 227–271). Dordrecht, The Netherlands: Springer.

Heiss, C., Ziegler, M., Engbert, K., Gropel, P., & Brand, R. (2010). Self-leadership and volition: Distinct and potentially supplemental constructs. *Psychological Reports, 107*(2), 447–462. doi:10.2466/01.03.07.14.

Hill, A. B., & Perkins, R. E. (1985). Towards a model of boredom. *British Journal of Psychology, 76*(2), 235–240. doi:10.1111/j.2044-8295.1985.tb01947.x.

Hollon, S. B., Haman, K. L., & Brown, L. L. (2002). Cognitive-behavioural treatment of depression. In I. H. Gotlib & C. L. Hammen (Eds.), *Handbook of depression* (pp. 383–403). New York, NY: The Guilford Press.

Hulleman, C. S., & Harackiewicz, J. M. (2009). Making education relevant: Increasing interest and performance in high school science classes. *Science, 326*, 1410–1412. doi:10.1126/science.1177067.

Inzlicht, M., & Schmeichel, B. J. (2012). What is ego depletion? Toward a mechanistic revision of the Resource Model of Self-Control. *Perspectives on Psychological Science, 7*(5), 450–463. doi:10.1177/1745691612454134.

Izard, C. E. (2009). Emotion theory and research: Highlights, unanswered questions, and emerging issues. *Annual Review of Psychology, 60*, 1–25. doi:10.1146/annurev.psych.60.110707.163539.

Izard, C. E., & Ackerman, B. P. (2000). Motivational, organizational, and regulatory functions of discrete emotions. In M. Lewis & J. Haviland-Jones (Eds.), *Handbook of emotions* (2nd ed., pp. 253–322). New York, NY: Guilford Press.

Järvelä, S., Järvenoja, H., Malmberg, J., & Hadwin, A. F. (2013). Exploring socially shared regulation in the context of collaboration. *Journal of Cognitive Education and Psychology, 12*(3), 67–286. doi:10.1891/1945-8959.12.3.267.

Järvenoja, H. (2010). *Socially shared regulation of motivation and emotions in collaborative learning* (Doctoral dissertation, University of Oulu, Oulu, Finland).

Jarvis, S., & Seifert, T. (2002). Work avoidance as a manifestation of hostility, helplessness, and boredom. *Alberta Journal of Educational Research, 48*(2), 2002, 174–187. Retrieved from http://ajer.synergiesprairies.ca

Jennings, J. (2012). *Reflections on a half-century of school reform: Why have we fallen short and where do we go from here?* Retrieved from http://www.cep-dc.org

Jervis, L. L., Spicer, P., & Manson, S. M. (2003). Boredom, 'trouble', and the realities of postcolonial reservation life. *Journal of the Society for Psychological Anthropology, 31*(1), 38–58. doi:10.1525/eth.2003.31.1.38.

Jha, A. P., Krompinger, J., & Baime, M. J. (2007). Mindfulness training modifies subsystems of attention. *Cognitive, Affective, & Behavioral Neuroscience, 7*(2), 109–119. doi:10.3758/CABN.7.2.109.

Johnson, R., Johnson, R., & Holubec, E. (1992). *Advanced cooperative learning.* Edina, MN: Interaction Book Company.

Jordan, A. H., & Lovett, B. J. (2007). Stereotype threat and test performance: A primer for school psychologists. *Journal of School Psychology, 45*, 45–59. doi:10.1016/j.jsp.2006.09.003.

Kane, M. J., & McVay, J. C. (2012). What mind wandering reveals about executive-control abilities and failures. *Current Directions in Psychological Science, 21*, 348–354. doi:10.1177/0963721412454875.

Kass, S. J., Vodanovich, S. J., & Callender, A. (2001). State-trait boredom: Relationship to absenteeism, tenure, and job satisfaction. *Journal of Business and Psychology, 16*(2), 317–326. doi:10.1023/A:1011121503118.

Kass, S. J., Wallace, J. C., & Vodanovich, S. J. (2003). Boredom proneness and sleep disorders as predictors of adult attention deficit scores. *Journal of Attention Disorders, 7*, 83–91. doi:10.1177/108705470300700202.

Kelly, M. (2010). The role of theory in qualitative health research. *Family Practice, 27*(3), 285–290. doi:10.1093/fampra/cmp077.

Keltner, D., & Gross, J. J. (1999). Functional accounts of emotions. *Cognition and Emotion, 13*(5), 467–480. doi:10.1080/026999399379140.

King, R. B., McInerney, D. M., & Watkins, D. A. (2012). How you think about your intelligence determines how you feel in school: The role of theories of intelligence on academic emotions. *Learning and Individual Differences, 22*(6), 814–819. doi:10.1016/j.lindif.2012.04.005.

Kogachi, K. (2013). *The antecedents and consequences of ethnically diverse early adolescents' school belonging and academic identity in middle school* (Thesis, University of California, Los Angeles, Los Angeles, CA).

Koretz, D., Barron, S., Mitchell, K., & Stecher, B. (1996). *The perceived effects of the Kentucky Instructional Results System (KIRIS).* Santa Monica, CA: RAND.

Kunter, M., & Baumert, J. (2006). Who is the expert? Construct and criteria validity of student and teacher ratings of instruction. *Learning Environments Research, 9*, 231–251. doi:10.1007/s10984-006-9015-7.

Lam, S., Wong, B. P. H., Yang, H., & Lui, Y. (2012). Understanding student engagement with a contextual model. In S. L. Christenson, A. L. Reschly, & C. Wylie (Eds.), *Handbook of research on student engagement* (pp. 403–419). New York, NY: Springer.

Larson, R. W., & Richards, M. H. (1991). Boredom in the middle school years: Blaming schools versus blaming students. *American Journal of Education, 99*(4), 418–433. doi:10.1086/443992.

Lavasani, M. G., Sharifian, M. S., Naghizadeh, S., & Hematirad, G. (2012). The effect of attribution retraining on academic achievement. *Procedia—Social and Behavioral Sciences, 46*, 5845–5848. doi:10.1016/j.sbspro.2012.06.526.

Leong, F. T. L., & Schneller, G. R. (1993). Boredom proneness: Temperamental and cognitive components. *Personality and Individual Differences, 14*, 4233–4239. doi:10.1016/0191-8869(93)90193-7.

LePera, N. (2011). Relationships between boredom proneness, mindfulness, anxiety, depression, and substance use. *The New School Psychology Bulletin, 8*(2), 15–25. doi:10.24z66/PMS.71.7.963-966.

Lichtenfeld, S., Pekrun, R., Stupnisky, R. H., Reiss, K., & Murayama, K. (2012). Measuring students' emotions in the early years: The Achievement Emotions Questionnaire-Elementary School (AEQ-ES). *Learning and Individual Differences, 22*(2), 190–201. doi:10.1016/j.lindif.2011.04.009.

Lipnevich, A. A., & Roberts, R. D. (2012). Noncognitive skills in education: Emerging research and applications in a variety of international contexts. *Learning and Individual Differences, 22*, 173–177. doi:10.1016/j.lindif.2011.11.016.

Macklem, G. L. (2014). *Preventive mental health at school: Evidence-based services for students.* New York, NY: Springer.

MacLean, K. A., Ferrer, E., Aichele, S. R., Bridwell, D. A., Zanesco, A. P., Jacobs, T. L., … Saron, C. D. (2010). Intensive meditation training improves perceptual discrimination and sustained attention. *Psychological Science, 21*(6), 829–839. doi:10.1177/0956797610371339.

Mahatmya, D., Lohman, B. J., Matjasko, J. L., & Farb, A. F. (2012). Engagement across developmental periods. In S. L. Christenson, A. L. Reschly, & C. Wylie (Eds.), *Handbook of research on student engagement* (pp. 45–63). New York, NY: Springer.

Malkovsky, E., Merrifield, C., Goldberg, Y., & Danckert, J. (2012). Exploring the relationship between boredom and sustained attention. *Experimental Brain Research, 221*(1), 59–67. doi:10.1007/s00221-012-3147.

Mallett, R. K., Mello, Z. R., Wagner, D. E., Worrell, F., Burrow, R. N., & Andretta, J. R. (2011). Do I belong?: It depends on when you ask. *Cultural Diversity & Ethnic Minority Psychology, 17*(4), 432–436. doi:10.1037/a0025455.

Maloney, E. A., Risko, E. F., Ansari, D., & Fugelsang, J. (2010). Mathematics anxiety affects counting but not subitizing during visual enumeration. *Cognition, 114*, 293–297. doi:10.1016/j.cognition.2009.09.013.

Manna, G., Faraci, P., & Como, M. R. (2013). Factorial structure and psychometric properties of the Sensation Seeking Scale—Form V (SSS-V) in a sample of Italian adolescents. *Europe's Journal of Psychology, 9*(2), 276–288. doi:10.5964/ejop.v9i2.500.

Marks, H. M. (2000). Student engagement instructional activity: Patterns in the elementary, middle, and high school years. *American Educational Research Journal, 37*(1), 153–184. doi:10.3102/00028312037001153.

Martin, A. J. (2012). Part II commentary: Motivation and engagement: Conceptual, operational, and empirical clarity. In S. L. Christenson, A. L. Reschly, & C. Wylie (Eds.), *Handbook of research on student engagement* (pp. 303–311). New York, NY: Springer.

Martin, A. J., Anderson, J., Bobis, J., Way, J., & Vellar, R. (2012). Switching on and switching off in mathematics: An ecological study of future intent and disengagement among middle school students. *Journal of Educational Psychology, 104*(1), 1–18. doi:10.1037/a0025988.

Martin, M., Sadlo, G., & Stew, G. (2006). The phenomenon of boredom. *Qualitative Research in Psychology, 3*, 193–211. doi:10.1191/1478088706qrp066oa.

Mazzone, L., Ducci, F., Scoto, M. C., Passaniti, E., D'Arrigo, V. G., & Vitiello, B. (2007). The role of anxiety symptoms in school performance in a community sample of children and adolescents. *BMC Public Health, 7*, 346. doi:10.1186/1471-2458-7-347.

McCann, E. J., & Turner, J. E. (2004). Increasing student learning through volitional control. *Teachers College Record, 106*(9), 1695–1714. doi:10.1111/j.1467-9620.2004.00401.x.

McGinnis, E., & Goldstein, A. P. (1997). *Skillstreaming the elementary school child: New strategies and perspectives for teaching prosocial skills.* Champaign, IL: Research Press.

McGrew, K. S. (2013). *The Motivation & Academic Competence (MACM) Commitment Pathway to Learning Model: Crossing the rubicon to learning action* (MindHub Pub. #1 2-23-13). Retrieved from http://www.iapsych.com

McIntosh, E. G. (2006). Sex differences in boredom proneness. *Psychological Reports, 98*, 625–626. doi:10.2466/pr0.98.3.625-626.

McKinney, A. A., Canu, W. H., & Schneider, H. G. (2013). Distinct ADHD symptom clusters differentially associated with personality traits. *Journal of Attention Disorders, 17*, 358–366. doi:10.1177/1087054711430842.

Mega, C., Ronconi, L., & DeBeni, R. (2013). What makes a good student? How emotions, self-regulated learning and motivation contribute to academic achievement. *Journal of Educational Psychology, 106*(1), 121–131. doi:10.1037/a0033546.

Mercer, K. B. (2008). *The measurement of boredom: Differences between existing self-report scales* (Master's thesis, York University, Toronto, Canada). Retrieved from http://www.doc88.com/p-23974360444.html

Mercer-Lynn, K. B., Bar, R. J., & Eastwood, J. D. (2014). Causes of boredom: The person, the situation, or both? *Personality and Individual Differences, 56,* 122–126. doi:10.1016/j.paid.2013.08.034.

Mercer-Lynn, K. B., Flora, D. B., Fahlman, S. A., & Eastwood, J. D. (2011). The measurement of boredom: Differences between existing self-report scales. *Assessment, 20*(5), 585–596. doi:10.1177/1073191111408229.

Mercer-Lynn, K. B., Hunter, J. A., & Eastwood, J. D. (2013). Is trait boredom redundant? *Journal of Social and Clinical Psychology, 32*(8), 897–916. doi:10.1521/jscp.2013.32.8.897.

Merrifield, C., & Danckert, J. (2014). Characterizing the psychophysiological signature of boredom. *Experimental Brain Research, 232*(2), 481–491. doi:10.1007/s00221-013-3755-2.

Meyer, D. K., & Turner, J. C. (2006). Re-conceptualizing emotion and motivation to learn in classroom contexts. *Educational Psychology Review, 18*(4), 377–390. doi:10.1007/s10648-006-9032-1.

Michael, J. (2006). Where's the evidence that active learning works? *Advances in Physiology Education, 30*(4), 159–167. doi:10.1152/advan.00053.2006.

Mora, R. (2011). School is so boring: High-stakes testing and boredom at an urban middle school. *Perspectives on Urban Education, 9*(1). Retrieved from http://www.urbanedjournal.org

Mouratidis, A., Vansteenkiste, M., & Lens, W. (2009). Beyond positive and negative affect: Achievement goals and discrete emotions in the elementary physical education classroom. *Psychology of Sport and Exercise, 10*(3), 336–343. doi:10.1016/j.psychsport.2008.11.004.

Muis, K. R., & Duffy, M. C. (2013). Epistemic climate and epistemic change: Instruction designed to change students' beliefs and learning strategies and improve achievement. *Journal of Educational Psychology, 105*(1), 213–225. doi:10.1037/a0029690.

Nett, U. E., Goetz, T., & Daniels, L. M. (2010). What to do when feeling bored? Students' strategies for coping with boredom. *Learning and Individual Differences, 20*(6), 626–638. doi:10.1016/j.lindif.2010.09.004.

Nett, U. E., Goetz, T., & Hall, N. C. (2011). Coping with boredom in school: An experience sampling perspective. *Contemporary Educational Psychology, 36,* 49–59. doi:10.1016/j.cedpsych.2010.10.003.

Neu, J. (1998). Boring from within: Endogenous versus reactive boredom. In W. F. Flack & J. D. Laird (Eds.), *Emotions in psychopathology: Theory and research* (pp. 158–170). London, England: Oxford University Press.

Newell, S. E., Harries, P., & Ayers, S. (2012). Boredom proneness in a psychiatric inpatient population. *International Journal of Social Psychology, 58*(5), 488–495. doi:10.1177/0020764011408655.

Opris, D., & Macavei, B. (2005). The distinction between functional and dysfunctional negative emotions: An empirical analysis. *Journal of Cognitive and Behavioral Psychotherapies, 5,* 181–195. Retrieved from https://www.babcp.com

Orcutt, J. D. (1984). Contrasting effects of two kinds of boredom on alcohol use. *Journal of Drug Issues, 14*(1), 161–173. doi:10.1037/a0032538.

Owens, M., Stevenson, J., Hadwin, J. A., & Norgate, R. (2012). When does anxiety help or hinder cognitive test performance? The role of working memory capacity. *British Journal of Psychology, 105*(1), 92–101. doi:10.1111/bjop.12009.

Padilla-Walker, L. M., Day, R. D., Dyer, W. J., & Black, B. C. (2013). "Keep on keeping on, even when it's hard!" Predictors and outcomes of adolescent persistence. *The Journal of Early Adolescence, 33*(4), 433–457. doi:10.1177/0272431612449387.

Papageorgiou, C., & Wells, A. (2000). Treatment of recurrent major depression with attention training. *Cognitive and Behavioral Practice, 7,* 407–413. doi:10.1016/S1077-7229(00)80051-6.

Parker, P. D., Prkachin, K. M., & Prkachin, G. C. (2005). Processing of facial expressions of negative emotion in alexithymia: The influence of temporal constraint. *Journal of Personality, 73*(4), 1087–1107. doi:10.1111/j.1467-6494.2005.00339.x.

Patall, E. A. (2013). Constructing motivation through choice, interest, and interestingness. *Journal of Educational Psychology, 105*(2), 522–534. doi:10.1037/a0030307.

Pekrun, R. (2006). The control-value theory of achievement emotions: Assumptions, corollaries, and implications for educational research and practice. *Educational Psychology Review, 18*(4), 315–341. doi:10.1007/s10648-006-9029-9.

Pekrun, R. (2007). Emotions in students' scholastic development. In R. P. Perry & J. C. Smart (Eds.), *The scholarship of teaching and learning in higher education: An evidence-based perspective* (pp. 553–610). Dordrecht, The Netherlands: Springer. doi:10.1007/1-4020-5742-3_13.

Pekrun, R., Elliot, A. J., & Maier, M. A. (2009). Achievement goals and achievement emotions: Testing a model of their joint relations with academic performance. *Journal of Educational Psychology, 101*(1), 115–135. doi:10.1037/a0013383.

Pekrun, R., Goetz, T., Daniels, L. M., Stupinsky, R. H., & Perry, R. P. (2010). Boredom in achievement settings: Exploring control–value antecedents and performance outcomes of a neglected emotion. *Journal of Educational Psychology, 102*(3), 531–549. doi:10.1037/a0019243.

Pekrun, R., Goetz, T., Frenzel, A. C., Barchfeld, P., & Perry, R. P. (2011). Measuring emotions in students' learning and performance: The Achievement Emotions Questionnaire (AEQ). *Contemporary Educational Psychology, 36*(1), 36–48. doi:10.1016/j.cedpsych.2010.10.002.

Pekrun, R., Goetz, T., Titz, W., & Perry, R. P. (2002). Academic emotions in students' self-regulated learning and achievement: A program of qualitative and quantitative research. *Educational Psychologist, 37*(2), 91–105. doi:10.1207/S15326985EP3702_4.

Pekrun, R., & Linnenbrink-Garcia, L. (2012). Academic emotions and student engagement. In S. L. Christenson, A. L. Reschly, & C. Wylie (Eds.), *Handbook of research on student engagement* (pp. 259–282). New York, NY: Springer.

Pekrun, R., & Stephens, E. J. (2009). Goals, emotions, and emotion regulation: Perspectives of the control-value theory. *Human Development, 52*, 357–365. doi:10.1159/000242349.

Perry, R. P., Stupinsky, R. H., Daniels, L. M., & Haynes, T. L. (2008). Attributional (explanatory) thinking about failure in new achievement settings. *European Journal of Education, 23*(4), 459–475. doi:10.1007/BF03172753.

Pfister, H., & Böhm, G. (2008). The multiplicity of emotions: A framework of emotional functions in decision making. *Judgment and Decision Making, 3*(1), 5–17. Retrieved from http://journal.sjdm.org

Pinzone, C. A., Appleton, J. J., & Reschly, A. L. (2014). *Longitudinal measurement invariance analysis of the Student Engagement Instrument-Brief (SEI-B)*. Poster presented at the National Association of School Psychologists Annual Convention—2014, Washington, DC.

Plucker, J. A., Robinson, N. M., Greenspon, T. S., Feldhusen, J. F., McCoach, D. B., & Subotnik, R. F. (2004). It's not how the pond makes you feel, but rather how high you can jump. *American Psychologist, 59*, 268–269. doi:10.1037/0003-066X.59.4.268.

Poon, D. C. H., & Leung, L. (2011). Effects of narcissism, leisure boredom, and gratifications sought on user-generated content among net-generation users. *International Journal of Cyber Behavior, Psychology and Learning, 1*(3), 1–14. doi:10.4018/ijcbpl.2011070101.

Preckel, F., Götz, T., & Frenzel, A. (2010). Ability grouping of gifted students: Effect on academic self-concept and boredom. *British Journal of Educational Psychology, 80*(3), 451–472. doi:10.1348/000709909X480716.

Prince, M. (2004). Does active learning work? A review of the research. *Journal of Engineering Education, 93*(3), 223–231. doi:10.1002/j.2168-9830.2004.tb00809.x.

Ratelle, C. F., Senècal, C., Vallerand, R. V., & Provencher, P. (2005). The relationship between school-leisure conflict and educational and mental health indexes: A motivational analysis. *Journal of Applied Social Psychology, 35*(9), 1800–1822. doi:10.1111/j.1559-1816.2005.tb02196.x.

Reschly, A. L., Huebner, E. S., Appleton, J. J., & Antaramian, S. (2008). Engagement as flourishing: The contribution of positive emotions and coping to adolescents' engagement at school and with learning. *Psychology in the Schools, 45*(5), 419–431. doi:10.1002/pits.20306.

Rieffe, C., & De Rooij, M. (2012). The longitudinal relationship between emotion awareness and internalising symptoms during late childhood. *European Child & Adolescent Psychiatry, 21*(6), 349–356. doi:10.1007/s00787-012-0267-8.

Rieffe, C., Oosterveld, P., & Terwogt, M. M. (2006). An alexithymia questionnaire for children: Factorial and concurrent validation results. *Personality and Individual Differences, 40*, 123–133. doi:10.1016/j.paid.2005.05.013.

Rimm-Kaufman, S. E., Larsen, R. A. A., Baroody, A. E., Curby, T. W., Ko, M., Thomas, J. B., … DeCoster, J. (2014). Efficacy of the responsive classroom approach: Results from a 3-year, longitudinal randomized controlled trial. *American Educational Research Journal, 51*(3), 567–603. doi:10.3102/0002831214523821.

Robertson, J. S. (2000). Is attribution training a worthwhile classroom intervention for K-12 students with learning difficulties? *Educational Psychology Review, 12*(1), 111–134. doi:10.1023/A:1009089118008.

Rogat, T. K., & Linnenbrink-Garcia, L. (2011). Socially shared regulation in collaborative groups: An analysis of the interplay between quality of social regulation and group processes. *Cognition and Instruction, 29*(4), 375–415. doi:10.1080/07370008.2011.607930.

Rupp, D. E., & Vodanovich, S. J. (1997). The role of boredom proneness in self-reported anger and aggression. *Journal of Social Behavior and Personality, 12*(4), 925–936.

Ruthig, J. C., Perry, R. P., Hall, N. C., & Hladkyj, S. (2004). Optimism and attributional retraining: Longitudinal effects on academic achievement, test anxiety, and voluntary course withdrawal in college students. *Journal of Applied Social Psychology, 34*(4), 709–730. doi:10.1111/j.1559-1816.2004.tb02566.x.

Sansone, C., & Thoman, D. B. (2005). Does what we feel affect what we learn? Some answers and new questions. *Learning and Instruction, 15*, 507–515. doi:10.1017/j.learninstruc.2005.07.015.

Sawin, D. A., & Scerbo, M. W. (1995). Effects of instruction type and boredom proneness in vigilance: Implications for boredom and workload. *Human Factors, 37*(4), 752–765. doi:10.1518/001872095778995616.

Schonert-Reichl, K. A., & Lawlor, M. S. (2010). The effects of a mindfulness-based education program on pre- and early adolescents' well-being and social and emotional competence. *Mindfulness, 1*, 137–151. doi:10.1007/s12671-010-0011-8.

Schonert-Reichl, K. A., Oberle, E., Lawlor, M. S., Abbott, D., Thomson, D., Oberlander, T., & Diamond, A. (2011). *Enhancing cognitive and social-emotional competence through a simple-to-administer school program.* Retrieved from http://discovermindfulness.ca

Schutz, P. A., & Lanehart, S. L. (2002). Introduction: Emotions in education. *Educational Psychologist, 37*, 67–68. doi:10.1207/S15326985EP3702_1.

Seifert, T. L. (1997). Academic goals and emotions: Results of a structural equation model and a cluster analysis. *British Journal of Educational Psychology, 67*(3), 323–338. doi:10.1111/j.2044-8279.1997.tb01247.x.

SEL Research Group/CASEL. (2010, Update). *The benefits of school-based social and emotional learning programs: Highlights from a major new report.* Retrieved from http://www.casel.org

Seo, M., Barrett, L. F., & Bartunek, J. M. (2004). The role of affective experience in work motivation. *The Academy of Management Review, 29*(3), 423–439. Retrieved from http://aom.org/amr/

Shaw, S. M., Caldwell, L. L., & Kleiber, D. A. (1996). Boredom, stress and social control in the daily activities of adolescents. *Journal of Leisure Research, 28*(4), 274–292. Retrieved from http://js.sagamorepub.com

Shernoff, D. J. (2013). *Optimal learning environments to promote student engagement.* New York, NY: Springer.

Shnabel, N., Purdie-Vaughns, V., Cook, J. E., Garcia, J., & Cohen, G. L. (2013). Demystifying values-affirmation interventions: Writing about social belonging is a key to buffering against identity threat. *Personality and Social Psychology Bulletin, 39*(5), 663–676. doi:10.1177/0146167213480816.

Siemer, E. A. (2009). Bored out of their minds: The detrimental effects of No Child Left Behind on gifted children. *Washington University Journal of Law & Policy, 30*(16), 539–560. Retrieved from http://digitalcommons.law.wustl.edu/wujlp/vol30/iss1/16

Skinner, E. A., & Belmont, M. J. (1993). Motivation in the classroom reciprocal effects of teacher behavior and student engagement across the school year. *Journal of Educational Psychology, 85*(4), 571–581. doi:10.1037/0022-0663.85.4.571.

Skinner, E., Furrer, C., Marchand, G., & Kindermann, T. (2008). Engagement and disaffection in the classroom: Part of a larger motivational dynamic? *Journal of Educational Psychology, 100*(4), 765–781. doi:10.1037/a0012840.

Smith, C. V., & Cardaciotto, L. (2011). Is active learning like broccoli? Student perceptions of active learning in large lecture classes. *Journal of the Scholarship of Teaching and Learning, 11*(1), 53–61. Retrieved from http://josotl.indiana.edu

Smith, M. L., & Rottenberg, C. (1991). Unintended consequences of external testing in elementary schools. *Educational Measurement: Issues and Practice, 10*(4), 7–11. doi:10.1111/j.1745-3992.1991.tb00210.x.

Smith, A., Taylor, E., Rogers, J. W., Newman, S., & Rubia, K. (2002). Evidence for a pure time perception deficit in children with ADHD. *Journal of Child Psychology and Psychiatry, 43*(4), 529–542. doi:10.1111/1469-7610.00043.

Sommers, J., & Vodanovich, S. J. (2000). Boredom proneness: Its relationship to psychological- and physical-health symptoms. *Journal of Clinical Psychology, 56*(1), 149–155. doi:10.1002/(SICI)1097-4679(200001)56:1<149::AID-JCLP14>3.0.

Suárez-Orozco, M. (2013, September 19). The elephant in the (class) room: Three ways to close the global education gap. *U.S. News Opinion.* Retrieved from http://www.usnews.com

Sucala, M., Scheckner, B., & David, D. (2010). Psychological time: Interval length judgments and subjective passage of time judgments. *Current Psychology Letters, 26*(2), 2–9. Retrieved from http://cpl.revues.org

Sundberg, N. D., Latkin, C. A., Farmer, R. F., & Saoud, J. (1991). Boredom in young adults: Gender and cultural comparisons. *Cross-Cultural Psychology, 22*(2), 209–223. doi:10.1177/0022022191222003.

Tabassam, W., & Grainger, J. (2002). Self-concept, attributional style and self-efficacy beliefs of students with learning disabilities with and without attention deficit hyperactivity disorder. *Learning Disability Quarterly, 25*(2), 141–152. doi:10.2307/1511280.

Tang, Y., Ma, Y., Wang, J., Fan, Y., Feng, S., Lu, Q., ... Posner, M. I. (2007). Short-term meditation training improves attention and self-regulation. *PNAS, 104*(43), 17152–17156. doi:10.1073/pnas.0707678104.

Tang, Y., & Posner, M. I. (2009). Attention training and attention state training. *Trends in Cognitive Science, 13*(5), 222–227. doi:10.1016/j.tics.2009.01.009.

Taylor, A. Z., & Graham, S. (2007). An examination of the relationship between achievement values and perceptions of barriers among low-SES African American and Latino students. *Journal of Educational Psychology, 99,* 52–64. doi:10.1037/0022-0663.99.1.52.

Thoman, D. B., Smith, J. L., Brown, E. R., Chase, J., & Lee, J. Y. K. (2013). Beyond performance: A motivational experiences model of stereotype threat. *Educational Psychology Review, 25*(2), 211–243. doi:10.1007/s10648-013-9219-1.

Thompson, S. (2001). The authentic standards movement and its evil twin. *Phi Delta Kappan, 82*(5), 358–362. doi:10.1177/003172170108200504.

Tobler, N. S., Roona, M. R., Ochshorn, P., Marshall, D. G., Streke, A. V., & Stackpole, K. M. (2000). School-based adolescent drug prevention programs: 1998 meta-analysis. *Journal of Primary Prevention, 20*(4), 275–336. doi:10.1023/A:1021314704811.

Todman, M. (2003). Boredom and psychotic disorders: Cognitive and motivational issues. *Psychiatry: Interpersonal and Biological Processes, 66*(2), 146–167. doi:10.1521/psyc.66.2.146.20623.

Todman, M. (2013). The dimensions of state boredom: Frequency, duration, unpleasantness, consequences and causal attributions. *Educational Research International, 1*(1), 32–40. Retrieved from http://erint.savap.org.pk/vol1n1.html

Torrente, F., Lischinsky, A., Torralva, T., Lopez, P., Roca, M., & Manes, F. (2011). Not always hyperactive? Elevated apathy scores in adolescents and adults with ADHD. *Journal of Attention Disorders, 15,* 545–556. doi:10.1177/1087054709359887.

Trautwein, U., Lüdtke, O., Kastens, C., & Köller, O. (2006). Effort on homework in grades 5–9: Development, motivational antecedents, and the association with effort on classwork. *Child Development, 77*(4), 1094–1111. doi:10.1111/j.1467-8624.2006.00921.x.

Triplett, C. F., Barksdale, M. A., & Leftwich, P. (2003). Children's perceptions of high stakes testing. *Journal of Research in Education, 13*(1), 15–21. Retrieved from http://www.eeraonline.org

Tulis, M., & Fulmer, S. M. (2013). Students' motivational and emotional experiences and their relationship to persistence during academic challenge in mathematics and reading. *Learning and Individual Differences, 27*, 35–46. doi:10.1016/j.lindif.2013.06.003.

Turner, J. E., & Husman, J. (2008). Emotional and cognitive self-regulation following academic shame. *Journal of Advanced Academics, 20*(1), 138–173. doi:10.4219/jaa-2008-864.

Tze, M. C. (2011). *Investigating academic boredom in Canadian and Chinese students* (Thesis, University of Alberta, Edmonton, Canada).

Tze, V. M. C., Klassen, R. M., Daniels, L. M., Li, J. C.-H., & Zhang, X. (2013). A cross-cultural validation of the Learning-Related Boredom Scale (LRBS) with Canadian and Chinese college students. *Journal of Psychoeducational Assessment, 31*, 29–39. doi:10.1177/0734282912443670.

Um, E., Plass, J. L., Hayward, E. O., & Homer, B. D. (2012). Emotional design in multimedia learning. *Journal of Educational Psychology, 104*(2), 485–498. doi:10.1037/a0026609.

Valiente, C., Swanson, J., & Eisenberg, J. (2012). Linking students' emotions and academic achievement: When and why emotions matter. *Child Development Perspectives, 6*(2), 129–135. doi:10.1111/j.1750-8606.2011.00192.x.

van Tilburg, W., & Igou, E. R. (2012). On boredom: Lack of challenge and meaning as distinct boredom experiences. *Motivation and Emotion, 36*(2), 181–194. doi:10.1007/s11031-011-9234-9.

Villavicencio, F. T., & Bernardo, A. B. I. (2013). Positive academic emotions moderate the relationship between self-regulation and achievement. *British Journal of Educational Psychology, 83*, 329–340. doi:10.0000/j/2044-8278.2012.02064.x.

Vodanovich, S. J. (2003). Psychometric measures of boredom: A review of the literature. *The Journal of Psychology, 137*(6), 569–595. doi:10.1080/00223980309600636.

Vodanovich, S. J., & Kass, S. J. (1990). A factor analytic study of the Boredom Proneness Scale. *Journal of Personality Assessment, 55*, 115–123. doi:10.1207/s15327752jpa5501&2_11.

Vodanovich, S. J., Kass, S. J., Andrasik, F., Gerber, W., Niederberger, U., & Breaux, C. (2011). Culture and gender differences in boredom proneness. *North American Journal of Psychology, 13*(2), 221. Retrieved from http://najp.us

Vodanovich, S. J., Verner, K. M., & Gilbride, T. V. (1991). Boredom proneness: Its relationship to positive and negative affect. *Psychological Reports, 69*, 1139–1146. doi:10.2466/pr0.1991.69.3f.1139.

Vodanovich, S. J., Wallace, J. C., & Kass, S. J. (2005). A confirmatory approach to the factor structure of the Boredom Proneness Scale: Evidence for a two-factor short form. *Journal of Personality Assessment, 85*(3), 295–303. doi:10.1207/s15327752jpa8503_05.

Vodanovich, S. J., Weddle, C., & Piotrowski, C. (1997). Relationship between boredom proneness and internal and external work values. *Social Behavior and Personality: An International Journal, 25*(3), 259–264. doi:10.2224/sbp.1997.25.3.259.

Vogel-Walcutt, J., Fiorella, L., Carper, T., & Schatz, S. (2012). The definition, assessment, and mitigation of state boredom within educational settings: A comprehensive review. *Educational Psychology Review, 24*(1), 89–111. doi:10.1007/s10648-011-9182-7.

Wallace, J. C., Vodanovich, S. J., & Restino, B. M. (2003). Predicting cognitive failures from boredom proneness and daytime sleepiness scores: An investigation within military and undergraduate samples. *Personality and Individual Differences, 34*(4), 635–644. doi:10.1016/S0191-8869(02)00050-8.

Wasson, A. S. (1981). Susceptibility to boredom and deviant behavior at school. *Psychological Reports, 48*, 901–902. doi:10.2466/pr0.1981.48.3.901.

Watt, J. D. (1991). Effect of boredom proneness on time perception. *Psychological Reports, 69*(1), 323–327. doi:10.2466/PR0.69.5.323-327.

Watt, J. D., & Hargis, M. B. (2010). Boredom proneness: Its relationship with subjective underemployment, perceived organizational support, and job performance. *Journal of Business and Psychology, 25*(1), 163–174. doi:10.1007/s10869-009-9138-9.

Watt, J. D., & Vodanovich, S. J. (1992). Relationship between boredom proneness and impulsivity. *Psychological Reports, 70*, 688–690. doi:10.2466/pr0.1992.70.3.688.

Way, I. F., Applegate, B., Cai, X., Franck, L. K., Black-Pond, C., Yelsma, P., ... Muliett, M. (2010). Children's Alexithymia Measure (CAM): A new instrument for screening difficulties with emotional expression. *Journal of Child & Adolescent Trauma, 3*(4), 303–318. doi:10.1080/193 61521.2010.523778.

Wegner, L., Flisher, A. J., Chikobvu, P., Lombard, C., & King, G. (2008). Leisure boredom and high school dropout in Cape Town, South Africa. *Journal of Adolescence, 31*(3), 421–431. doi:10.1016/j.adolescence.2007.09.004.

Weiner, B. (1985). An attributional theory of achievement motivation and emotion. *Psychological Review, 92*(4), 548–573. doi:10.1037/0033-295X.92.4.548.

Weir, K. (2013, July/August). Never a dull moment: Things get interesting when psychologists take a closer look at boredom. *Monitor on Psychology, 44*(7), 54. Retrieved from http://www. apa.org/monitor/2013/07-08/dull-moment

Willging, C. E., Quintero, G. A., & Lilliott, E. A. (2014). Hitting the wall: Youth perspectives on boredom, trouble, and drug use dynamics in rural New Mexico. *Youth & Society, 46*(1), 3–29. doi:10.1177/0044118x11423231.

Wittmann, M., & Paulis, M. P. (2008). Decision making, impulsivity and time perception. *Trends in Cognitive Science, 12*(1), 7–12. doi:10.1016/j.tics.2007.10.004.

Wolters, C. A., Pintrich, P. R., & Karabenick, S. A. (2003). *Assessing academic self-regulation learning.* Paper prepared for the Conference on Indicators of Positive Development: Definitions, Measures, and Prospective Validity. Sponsored by ChildTrends, National Institutes of Health.

Wolters, C. A., & Rosenthal, H. (2000). The relation between student's motivational beliefs and their use of motivational regulation strategies. *International Journal of Educational Research, 33*, 801–820. doi:10.1016/S0883-0355(00)00051-3.

Wolters, C. A., & Taylor, D. J. (2012). A self-regulated learning perspective on student engagement. In S. L. Christenson, A. L. Reschly, & C. Wylie (Eds.), *Handbook of research on student engagement* (pp. 635–651). New York, NY: Springer.

Wood, J. (2006). Effect of anxiety reduction on children's school performance and social adjustment. *Developmental Psychology, 42*(2), 345–349. doi:10.1037/0012-1649.42.2.345. 345.

Woolf, B. P., Arroyo, I., Muldner, K., Burleson, W., Cooper, D., Dolan, R., & Christopherson, R. M. (2010). *The effect of motivational learning companions on low-achieving students and students with learning disabilities.* International Conference on Intelligent Tutoring Systems, 2010, Pittsburgh, PA.

Wu, X., Anderson, R. C., Nguyen-Johiel, K., & Miller, B. (2013). Enhancing motivation and engagement through collaborative discussion. *Journal of Educational Psychology, 105*(3), 622–632. doi:10.1037/a0032792.

Yamac, A. (2014). Classroom emotions scale for elementary school students (Ces-Ess). *Mevlana International Journal of Education, 4*(1), 150–163. doi:10.13054/mije.13.72.4.1.

Yan, D., & Guoliang, Y. (2007). The development and application of an academic emotions questionnaire (Abstract). *Acta Psychologica Sinica, 39*(5), 852–860. Retrieved from http://118.145.16.229:81/Jweb_xlxb/EN/Y2007/V39/105/852

Yazzie-Mintz, E. (2010, June). *Charting the path from engagement to achievement: A report on the 2009 high school survey of student engagement.* Bloomington, IN: Indiana University Center for Evaluation and Education Policy (CEEP). Retrieved from http://hub.mspnet.org/index. cfm/20806

Yeager, S. D., & Bundick, M. J. (2009). The role of purposeful work goals in promoting meaning in life and in schoolwork during adolescence. *Journal of Adolescent Research, 24*, 423–452. doi:10.1177/0743558409336749.

Yeager, D. S., Henderson, M., D'Mello, S., Paunesku, D., Walton, G. M., Spitzer, B. J., & Duckworth, A. L. (2014, March). *Boring but important: A self-transcendent purpose for learning fosters academic self-regulation.* Retrieved from http://web.stanford.edu/~gwalton/home/ Welcome_files/Yeager_etal_inpress.pdf

Yeager, D. S., & Walton, G. M. (2011). Social-psychological interventions in education: They're not magic. *Review of Educational Research, 81,* 267–301. doi:10.3102/0034654311405999.

Zeidner, M. (1996). How do high school and college students cope with test situations? *British Journal of Educational Psychology, 66*(1), 115–128. doi:10.1111/j.2044-8279.1996.tb01181.x.

Zuckerman, M. (1979). *Sensation seeking: Beyond the optimal level of arousal.* Hillsdale, NJ: Erlbaum.

Zuckerman, M. (2007). The Sensation Seeking Scale V (SSS-V): Still reliable and valid. *Personality and Individual Differences, 43*(5), 1303–1305. doi:10.1016/j.paid.2007.03.021.

Zuckerman, M., Eysenck, S. B. J., & Eysenck, H. J. (1978). Sensation seeking in England and America: Cross-cultural, age, and sex comparisons. *Journal of Consulting and Clinical Psychology, 46*(1), 139–149. doi:10.1037/0022-006X.46.1.139.

Zuckerman, M., Kolin, E. A., Price, L., & Zoob, I. (1964). Development of a sensation-seeking scale. *Journal of Consulting Psychology, 28*(6), 477–482. doi:10.1037/h0040995.

Zusho, A., Pintrich, P. R., & Cortina, K. A. (2005). Motives, goals, and adaptive patterns of performance in Asian American and Anglo American students. *Learning and Individual Differences, 15*(2), 141–158. doi:10.1016/j.lindif.2004.11.003.

CPSIA information can be obtained at www.ICGtesting.com
Printed in the USA
BVOW09s0121090115

382607BV00002BA/5/P